TRAVELLERS
OF THE HEART

Text copyright © Michael Mitton 2013
The author asserts the moral right
to be identified as the author of this work

Published by
The Bible Reading Fellowship
15 The Chambers, Vineyard
Abingdon OX14 3FE
United Kingdom
Tel: +44 (0)1865 319700
Email: enquiries@brf.org.uk
Website: www.brf.org.uk
BRF is a Registered Charity

ISBN 978 0 85746 221 3

First published 2013

10 9 8 7 6 5 4 3 2 1 0

Acknowledgments

Unless otherwise stated, scripture quotations are taken from the New Revised Standard
Version of the Bible, Anglicised Edition, copyright © 1989, 1995 by the Division of Christian
Education of the National Council of the Churches of Christ in the United States of America,
and are used by permission. All rights reserved.

Scripture taken from the Holy Bible, New International Reader's Version®.Copyright © 1996,
1998 Biblica. All rights reserved throughout the world. Used by permission of Biblica.

The paper used in the production of this publication was supplied by mills that source their
raw materials from sustainably managed forests. Soy-based inks were used in its printing and
the laminate film is biodegradable.

A catalogue record for this book is available from the British Library

Printed in Singapore by Craft Print International Ltd

TRAVELLERS
OF THE HEART

MICHAEL
MITTON

**EXPLORING
NEW PATHWAYS
ON OUR SPIRITUAL
JOURNEY**

To Julia
my beloved and faithful travelling companion

Contents

Chapter 1

The call to travel

*Now the Lord said to Abram, 'Go from your country and your
kindred and your father's house to the land that I will show
you. I will make of you a great nation, and I will bless you,
and make your name great, so that you will be a blessing.
I will bless those who bless you, and the one who curses you
I will curse; and in you all the families of the earth shall be
blessed.'*
GENESIS 12:1–3

There is a great deal of travelling in the early chapters of Genesis.
Adam and Eve were forced to travel from their settled and blessed
land of paradise; Cain became a fugitive and a wanderer because
of his murder of Abel; Noah travelled in his great boat to Mount
Ararat, not because he planned a visit there but because, if he
wanted to stay alive, he had no choice but to board that boat
and go wherever the floodwaters took it; and the people of Babel
travelled because they had foolishly attempted to become like God
and, as a result, were scattered over the face of the earth.

In these early chapters of Genesis there is a great restlessness due
to human sinfulness and folly, and by the time you reach chapter
12 you are pretty exhausted by it all. Then we come to Abram, a
man who was by all accounts a good deal better and holier than
the motley crowd of humans that we encountered in the earlier
chapters. But if we think this means that at last someone is going to

settle down, we will be wrong. For Abraham (as he becomes) is the first truly great intentional traveller, and he does not travel because he is being exiled or punished, or to escape flood waters or Babel towers. He moves because of a calling, and it is a calling from the Most High.

Abraham, we are told a few millennia later by another great traveller, Paul, was a man of beautiful, simple, rugged and holy faith (Romans 4) and his travelling came from his desire simply to do what God asked of him. If we scan the pages of both Old and New Testaments, we see stories of many others who travelled in their desire to do what God had told them—Moses, Joshua, Ezra and Jonah, to name but a few. When we arrive at the New Testament and are introduced to Jesus, it is not surprising to find that he too is a traveller. Not only does he take the most momentous journey from heaven to earth, but, once on earth and into the stride of his earthly ministry, he journeys through Galilee and Judah, and even over the borders from time to time, to declare and demonstrate the wonderful good news of the kingdom of God. After the Gospels, we have the book of Acts, and there we find more people on journeys, such as Philip travelling to the desert (Acts 8:26–40) and, of course, the restless Paul, who made three great missionary journeys and ended his life in Rome, having travelled thousands of miles to share the gospel of Christ.

It may not altogether surprise us to hear about all of this travelling in the Bible, because so many great adventure stories involve travel. Take, for example, one of the epic stories of our time, Tolkien's *The Lord of the Rings*, which is a travelling story from beginning to end, in which Frodo and his companions make the hazardous journey from the Shire to Mount Doom and back again. And if that is not enough, the story finishes with Frodo and a few others making a further, much more mysterious journey to the Grey Havens, introducing another dimension of travel. Such stories instinctively move us because the desire to explore, travel and discover is deep in the human spirit.

There is so much that can cause us to want to travel—curiosity, a need to escape, a longing for adventure, unspecific restlessness, boredom or, as in the case of Abraham, a sense of calling from God. Whatever the driver, many of us find ourselves travellers in this world. Some are literal travellers: they move around a lot geographically, always having another journey up their sleeves and on the look-out for new parts of the planet to explore. Others are less literal travellers—what we might call 'travellers of the heart'. They may experience all the same kinds of motivations that cause the physical travellers to get up and go to places, but the type of journeying is different.

For many people, of course, the two types of travelling go hand in hand, and this was true of Abraham. Every inch of his journey from Ur of the Chaldees to the promised land was matched by a parallel journey of discovering God. The God who spoke to him at the start of his journey appeared to be fairly straightforward, if pretty demanding, but, as Abraham journeyed on, he discovered him to be a God who was not at all straightforward. This God kept Abraham guessing by taking his time to fulfil the promises of children and land, caused a 'thick and terrible darkness' to come over him (Genesis 15:12, NIRV) when he might have expected quite the opposite, and even led him up a terrible path that appeared to be leading him to murder his son. As Abraham strode on down the dusty pathways to new lands, he became increasingly aware that God was leading him on journeys of the heart that at one time he would never have imagined possible.

Those who go on walking pilgrimages often testify to this parallel travelling. The 'outer' journey is about things like physical strength, footwear, weather conditions, navigation and resting places, but most pilgrims testify to the fact that as they walk the outer journey, all the while there is an 'inner' journey taking place. South African Bishop Eric Pike and his wife Joyce walked the Camino de Santiago de Compostela in Northern Spain in 2010, and, in writing about the experience of this 600-mile walk, he observed:

For us the pilgrimage was not about the distance we walked, nor the destination, though these were important elements in our Camino. What was, and is important, is what God did in us along the way in terms of transformation, cleansing and purifying. The blisters heal, the aching shoulders are restored, but what endures is the reality of the encounters with the ever present and gracious God.[1]

Pilgrimages are increasingly popular but not many of us will be regular pilgrims. However, all of us embark on a pilgrimage through life from the moment we are born. Like any pilgrimage, this journey has a beginning, a destination, resting places and untold numbers of discoveries, problems and encounters along the way. Just like the pilgrims trekking intentionally to a holy place, we are making our journey through this precious life of ours to our final destination of heaven. On this journey we also have a choice: we can put our heads down and march forward from the beginning of one day to its end, day after day, doing our errands, ticking off our checklists and generally getting the journey done as efficiently as possible, or we can travel in a more alert and attentive way, giving time and space to being aware of the journey of the heart. We can pause on our journey and take a look at the terrain around us, reflecting on the road we have travelled, making choices about the roads ahead of us, and thinking about the people we have been meeting on the way. As we do so, we see that our journey through life is full of fascinating twists and turns, encounters, discoveries, choices, gains, losses, highs and lows as well as a fair bit of the mundane and apparently ordinary.

It is this journey that I want to explore in this book, looking in particular at important influences that give our journey a sense of direction. There could be any number of ways of approaching this subject, but the one I have chosen is to work with my own personal experience and to explore the variety of spiritualities and traditions that I have either stumbled upon or deliberately explored in my travels of the heart over the years. It is always dangerous to share our own experience, for it can too easily appear that we are being prescriptive for others or setting ourselves up as a kind of model that all should follow. I should be horrified if I succeeded in achieving either of these ends! However, I feel it is worth taking a risk in telling my story, because the best tutors to me over the years have been those who have been prepared to share their stories, their testimonies, their ups and downs of life, their struggles and discoveries. Often their experiences have been very different from my own, but as I listen to them, they help me reflect on what is taking place in me. They become, if you like, contemporary parables for me.

Jesus favoured the use of parables. His stories enabled people to think about how they were living their lives. It didn't matter whether or not they had the same experience as the one described in the parable. Simply by listening, they found themselves reflecting on their own lives. So, for example, few people listening to the parable of the good Samaritan would have been able to say, 'Exactly the same thing happened to me last week when I was going down to Jericho.' Yet even 2000 years later, we read that parable and find ourselves asking questions about how we treat our fellow humans. This is the point of sharing stories: not to get others to copy us but to open each other's minds to possibilities and to reflect on what is happening in our lives. There is, I suppose, an equivalent in watching someone else's holiday film. It can be pretty dull if we are simply observers of another person's experience, but it becomes wonderful when we find something stirring inside that says, 'It's time I did some travelling!' So as I share some of my discoveries, with snapshots of what I have discovered along the way, I hope that you will be helped to reflect on your own travels of the heart, and that you may feel inspired to make further explorations on your journey.

In my book *Dreaming of Home*, I wrote about the homing instinct that I believe lies within all of us—an instinct that searches for a place of belonging, a place where we can be truly ourselves without fear or shame, a place where at last we can feel beloved on the earth. I want to hold firm to that homing instinct as I explore the theme of travelling in the heart. Many people find themselves exploring a particular spirituality because they are drawn to some aspect of it that feels like home. I have noticed that this is particularly true of Celtic spirituality. But while an encounter with a particular spirituality might feel as if it is drawing some people closer to their true home and place of belonging, for other people it could have quite the opposite effect. One very good yardstick for measuring whether a particular spirituality is going to be helpful is to see if it encourages you to become more fully 'you'.

There are many 'dechurched' people (those who once attended church regularly but have now left) who were attracted into a Christian spirituality, or a particular expressions of that spirituality, that eventually led them away from their true homeland rather than drawing them towards being more fully themselves. For them, such a tension becomes unbearable and they end up having to leave the church, often not knowing where to look next for their longed-for spiritual homeland. It seems to me that all spiritualities offer us great possibilities for either discovering or losing ourselves, and so the journey is filled with both adventure and risk. It is, therefore, a journey on which we need the companionship of the Holy Spirit, who leads us into truth (John 16:13).

As I reflect on my six decades in this world, I realise that I have explored a reasonable range of Christian spiritualities, and in this book I identify seven that have been important for me. The choice is by no means comprehensive and is very subjective. Let me repeat: I am writing about my own experience, and my hope is that in reading about it you will be encouraged to reflect on your journey and feel stirred to explore new pathways of your own.

To stay with the theme of travelling, I imagined what these spiritualities would be like if they were part of a British landscape that I was traversing. The *Anglicanism* into which I was born, and in which I have served as a priest for over 30 years, looked like a wide open plain, solid and dependable ground, secure enough to hold many habitations. *Evangelicalism* was the spirituality that brought my faith alive as a youngster, and that, to me, looked like the home counties, where I grew up. The *charismatic* experience that took me by surprise in my late teens and has been important to me ever since looked like a rushing stream, full of life and energy and delight but also menace—a bit risky and messy.

I encountered *catholic* spirituality mainly through good friends (both Roman Catholics and Anglo-Catholics) and I saw this spirituality as a kind of hilly border region, where I was being led into territories that felt different, sometimes even foreign, and yet full of interest. I saw *Celtic* spirituality as a range of Irish, Scottish or Welsh mountains, and I also thought of the Malvern Hills over which I walked many times when I lived in Worcestershire. These are apparently the most ancient of mountains, and the Celtic ways are ancient ways, as well as ways of great strength.

Then I had to consider *liberalism*, and I saw this terrain as marshlands, partly because I'm not so familiar with marshlands and partly because they feel to me a little dangerous. But although they seem dangerous, this is no excuse for not exploring, and I have discovered some wonderful wildlife in these lands that once held only threats for me. Finally I wanted to include some of the new life that I am finding in my work with *Fresh Expressions*. I saw this as the coastal regions, because here the known land ends and the seas begin. Here we are introduced to a very different terrain, where we find the spiritualities of the unchurched, which are very diverse and interesting.

I want to emphasise again that this is entirely *my* experience, and others doing this exercise will find that different terrains and landscapes come to mind as they consider their spiritual travels.

The final chapter of this book is called 'Rest and be thankful'. Some years ago, my wife Julia and I visited Iona and the area of Scotland around that special island. When we drove back to Glasgow Airport from Oban, we stopped at the wonderfully named

'Rest and Be Thankful' spot on the A83. Here you can stop the car to rest on your journey and look out on the most wonderful view (on a good day!). So, at the end of the book, I want to do the same—to pause on the journey, take a look at the view and, with gratitude, think of the ground we have covered. I will also draw together some principles that are important for this kind of travelling.

For many years I was fortunate to enjoy the friendship of Brother Ramon SSF, who died in 2000. Ramon consistently inspired me to be a heart-traveller. He grew up in Wales and came from a strong Welsh Baptist faith-fuelled family, but, as time went on, he discovered other spiritualities including Pentecostalism, Anglicanism, Franciscan spirituality and the complex of spiritualities within the mystical tradition. What I really admired about Ramon was the fact that he never jettisoned an 'old' spirituality in order to explore a new one. He would often say that he was a liberal catholic charismatic evangelical ecumenical Anglican—and he was!

It seems to me that Ramon modelled the right kind of travelling: he took the risk of exploring spiritualities that were new to him, and he made space for them not by throwing out the old ones but by growing as a person to accommodate the new. For him, the really important thing was that every spirituality should be a servant, helping to steer us in the direction of Jesus. The real danger came if they became lords of us and distracted us from Jesus. Any of these spiritualities can become like controlling powers, and we get stuck in awkward loyalty traps, feeling that we must toe party lines, impress party leaders and generally show ourselves to be true party members by adopting party language and styles of behaviour. In all our explorations, therefore, we will need to keep asking the same question: is this a path that will lead me closer to Jesus?

Even that simple language betrays a particular spirituality. I can see some of you flinch a little, as it sounds a bit too evangelical, while others might feel it isn't quite strong enough for their taste. It is impossible to find language that doesn't smack of one tradition or another, and in the end we simply have to be true to ourselves. I think, though, that whichever spiritualities have instinctively been home for us, we do have a common bond, which is that we long to love the Lord our God with all our hearts, and our neighbours as ourselves. In the pages of the Gospels we find the one who has touched our hearts more than any other, who is the very reason why we are on this journey in the first place, and is the destination for which we yearn. In the final chapter of his book *Pilgrimage*, Andrew Jones writes, 'Pilgrimage is ultimately about progressing into the heart of God.'[2]

Finally a word about terminology: it has been hard to work out whether to use the word 'tradition' or 'spirituality' to describe particular expressions of our faith. Generally speaking, I choose 'spirituality' but, because one word can start to sound tedious when it is overused, I sometimes use 'tradition'. To be honest, I find that no word is really adequate, and I acknowledge that 'spirituality' has limited value, not least because there is much more to spirituality than particular ways of expressing our faith. The good thing about this particular word, though, is that it has the word 'spirit' at its heart, and what I am writing about is an activity in our spirits, an activity that needs the blessed and fluent life of the Holy Spirit.

May that same Spirit now be our guide through the plains and home counties, along streams and by borders, up mountains and over fenlands, and on to the coastlands. There, perhaps more than anywhere else, we stand a good chance of witnessing the Spirit of God, who, at the very beginning of the journey of this world, moved over the face of the waters with such surprising and energising life.

Chapter 2

Anglican plains

There is something indelibly Anglican in my soul. It's there as much by inheritance as anything else. Around the time I was training for ordination, my Uncle Jack Mitton contacted me. He lived with his daughter, Primrose, in Matlock, Derbyshire, and I had known him since childhood. A veteran of World War I, he used to delight in telling us that he escaped death in the trenches one night simply by choosing to go to the toilet at the right time. On returning to his night shelter, he found it demolished by an enemy shell. It was probably the violent noise of those trenches that left him fairly deaf, so any conversation with Jack had to be carried out at high volume.

Even in his late 80s he would drive the long journey to our family home in his Austin Cambridge and, during his summer visits, he would play cricket with me on the back lawn. We were, in a rather formal way, very fond of each other, and I felt touched when he announced one day that he had chosen to make me 'Custodian of the Family Memoirs', a duty I was delighted to accept. I still have in my loft four large boxes of assorted files, all detailing various bits of Mitton history, but among the volumes of paperwork and obscure books, he also passed my way photos of portraits of ancient relatives, most of whom seemed to be Anglican clergy. As a young man delighting in a much more carefree charismatic life, I wasn't altogether taken with these images of serious-faced, heavily robed clerics. Yet I had to acknowledge that, despite a couple of generations of secular Mittons immediately before me, when

I reached back to my great-grandfather I touched a long line of ancestors who, one after the other, were in holy orders and served in parishes in the north of England.

Although, as a young adult, I preferred to believe that I was completely uninfluenced by such a powerful and lengthy strain of Anglicanism in my family history, I now think it probably did have an influence, not least in giving me a sense of the Anglican Church being my natural, inherited church. I had very little interest in ancient ancestors at that time, whereas nowadays I do want to know something about them, perhaps because as we get older we seem to need to set our lives in the context of a wider story. Perhaps it is about finding a place of belonging in our family story and having some sense that we are playing a part in a longer story. In reflecting on our own spiritual journey, it is important to look back at our family history and see how faith found expression in that story, and what particular spiritual traditions influenced the family over the years. I have come across people who are now leaders of out-and-out free and independent churches who speak quite wistfully of their family roots in one of the main denominational churches. In the heyday of modernism in the 1960s and '70s it was the fashion to lampoon these churches, but now, in our postmodern era, owning a connection to a historic church denomination invites much less ridicule. This has perhaps made it easier for Free Church people to integrate their family story. It may even explain why some independent church leaders and members display a real affection for churches such as the Anglican Church, and quite a number even make their way back to it. Of course, a reverse journey could also be made: an Anglican worshipper may feel drawn back to a family affiliation with nonconformist churches.

My Uncle Jack liked to imagine that he had traced our family back to William the Conqueror, but I think this was more romantic and wishful thinking than the fruit of accurate research. However, he did succeed in tracking us back to a certain Robert Mitton who was baptised in 1629. Robert's son Roger is the first vicar to appear in our family records, and he had the cure of souls in parishes in York and Skipton less than 40 years after the publication of the Book of Common Prayer. If I could line up all these parsons in my family history, what an interesting story of Anglican life they could tell me!

Anglicanism is a tradition that includes all those churches across the world that have a connection with the Church of England. It is an extraordinarily broad church and during my life I have had contact with a fair bit of it. I have walked for several hours down long grassy tracks to preach in remote Anglican churches in rural Kenya and I have prayed in incense-filled churches in South African townships; I have sung charismatic worship in St Andrew's Cathedral of Singapore and experienced High Mass in Episcopal churches in the USA. I have co-celebrated at a Eucharist in Japan and I have baptised adults in a murky pool in South India. Most of my work overseas has been at the invitation of Anglican churches and there is something very moving about being welcomed not only as a fellow Christian but also as a fellow Anglican.

I have noticed that once a type of Anglican life has been established in a country, the worshippers are, generally speaking, inclined to keep close to the expression of Anglicanism that was first planted there. Thus, the Anglican Church in South Africa is predominantly Anglo-Catholic after the missionary work of the Mirfield Fathers, whereas in East Africa it is more Evangelical following the work of mission societies such as CMS. In the UK, though, the scene is completely different. Here the differences are extraordinary. You can go to one part of town and find an Anglican church that, to all intents and purposes, feels Roman Catholic, with the priests wearing Roman robes, and language and liturgy resonant of Roman Catholic worship; then, just down the road in the neighbouring parish, there is a church where the vicar rolls up in jeans and open-neck shirt, with no vestments in sight, the guitar-led band plays light rock music, and you might think you were in one of the new churches.

One of the distinctives of the Church of England is this breadth of life. Although held together by the four main essentials defined in the Lambeth Quadrilateral,[3] it is nonetheless able to express itself in great diversity. Of course, this diversity puts it under great strain as increasingly polarised views, particularly on human sexuality, stretch the unity of the Anglican Communion to possible breaking point. My sense is that in the UK we are better equipped to manage such diversity and can live better with difference. When my faith came alive in my late teens, for a time I was very intolerant of those forms of Anglicanism that varied from the type I loved. As I shall explain in the next chapter, I was most definitely evangelical and, as far as I was concerned, the liberal and high church expressions of the Church of England were to be resisted. There are still quite a number of British Anglicans who feel very strongly about their tradition today, but I notice that the majority have a generous heart and manage well this breadth of spirituality.

The breadth is not just about spiritual traditions, however. It also relates to the reach that the Church of England has into our communities. Although the parish system is under strain in this post-Christendom era, there is still enough memory to cause the unchurched majority to welcome clergy to school assemblies and other community activities, and to feel drawn to churches when there are national tragedies or special occasions such as Remembrance and Christmas.

So, for me, the Church of England was the starting point on my spiritual journey. All of us who grow up in churchgoing homes will develop a unique relationship to our particular church. The church we are taken to (or, in some cases, sent to) is our first experience of worship and, no matter how young we are, we will develop feelings about it. We will not only learn some general theology but we will also pick up the customs and beliefs of that particular church. For those early years, we will regard that type of church as 'normal', and we may well believe that all Christians follow their faith in that way. As a young child, as far as I was concerned there was no church other than the Church of England. As an infant growing up in Edinburgh, I was taken along to St John's Church on Princes Street and the routines of Anglican Sunday worship became as normal as the roast lunch afterwards and the walk up Blackford Hill in the afternoon.

When, at the age of seven, I moved with my family to the village of Great Missenden in Buckinghamshire, it came as no surprise that on our first Sunday morning we packed ourselves into the car and made the first of many trips through the village high street, up the little lane and over the new bypass to the Chiltern-flint church dedicated to the great saints Peter and Paul. There I would sit on the polished pinewood pew in my Sunday best and, as the ancient words from the ancient vicar drifted around the ancient church (and well above my young head), my mind happily drifted where it would and was seldom occupied by the subject-matter of the sermon, readings, prayers or hymns. The sense of antiquity was comforting in a way, but the rest of my life was being lived in the modern world of the 1960s, with its mix of threats and opportunities, and little that was said or sung in church seemed to bear much relation to that world.

Years later, I visited that church again and was taken aback by the wealth of emotion that was stirred in me as I entered the building. I had not set foot inside for over 40 years and, before entering, I could remember very little of it, but once inside I was astonished to discover how familiar the pews, windows, stone carvings, patterned flooring and other furnishings felt. As I sat there in the stained-glass filtered sunlight, I was taken back to my childhood days and felt once more the solid security of my father sitting next to me. What came back to me was a sense of sitting in a world that really belonged to others, in particular those who understood the words and those who managed to achieve some kind of connection with a past that felt much more like theirs than mine. Nonetheless, even then I had known without any doubt that there was a place for me in that building and among those people; while others in the congregation applied themselves to the words of hymns, prayers and sermons, those words became a comforting backdrop for me as my mind wandered, as it so frequently did in those days, to apparently unconnected thoughts and events. My eyes would roam around the beautiful building, and a kind of partnership built up between my thoughts and the carvings, windows, floors and arches. They were by no means unreligious thoughts, but in truth the religion I felt did not seem to have much to do with the religion practised by the grown-ups in that church.

Hours and hours of Sunday mornings and evenings were spent in this way, and so engraved on my mind were the impressions from that time that when I re-entered the building after 40 years, I felt I knew each and every stone, carving and window pane as a long-lost friend and experienced an extraordinary surge of affection for it all.

For any who have grown up in the Christian faith, I would strongly recommend trying to revisit the building where you worshipped in those formative days of childhood. There, memories can return that may well have been among your first religious experiences. For some, these may be very distinctive and spiritual memories, perhaps recalling a real awareness of the numinous holiness of God; for others, they may be memories of God's love, so strong that it almost seemed tangible; and for yet others, there may even have been revelations or visions. There will be some who recall singing hymns that they grew to love, and for others there may be bits of sermons that they remember, perhaps because the preacher spoke so precisely to a particular life situation that it left an indelible mark in the soul. And there will be some who return to the place of worship but, before they feel any remembrance of Sundays, meet head-on a sharper and less welcome memory of a family funeral. Then, the coldness and fear of those early days of grief can suddenly return as a sharp, wintery breeze.

Whatever we discover when we get there is likely to be valuable as we sit in the pew or seat, draw ourselves down to our deeper memories and explore what we find. We may well gain insights into the way our faith first found shape and language in our souls.

I was sent to a preparatory school in the nearby town of Amersham. At that school, there were brief acts of worship at the beginning and end of each day, when the headmaster would summon us to pray, always faithfully using the Anglican collects. Even though I have never been able to learn lines to save my life, the words of those collects have somehow stuck fast in me, so that when the season of Lent arrives, it is second nature for me to ask God to 'create and make in us new and contrite hearts, that we lamenting our sins and acknowledging our wretchedness may obtain of thee, the God of all mercy, perfect remission and forgiveness'. It never seemed to matter to me that I had little clue about the meaning of words like 'contrite' and 'remission'; somehow, my growing acquaintance with the words gave them a comforting quality. For me, church and school worship were occasions when there were no demands made and no real risk of being made to look foolish, where familiar words somehow managed to give me strength.

I don't often take Book of Common Prayer services now, but when I do, and when I start the Confession by acknowledging 'the devices and desires of our own hearts', I am instantly taken back in my mind and heart to those days in school and church. I don't think I'm alone in this experience, and I suspect that many of those who love Book of Common Prayer services have similar memories operating, and are reaching out to parts of their own personal history for safety and assurance. These are powerful emotions, and they are one of the reasons why leading a church into change can be so difficult. We can very easily dismiss such feelings as 'nostalgic', but humans have always drawn much strength from such experiences. To slash away at these memories without any reference to their value can cause enormous pain to people. If such services have to leave our regular patterns of worship, proper care has to be given to the passing of these old rites, so that those who draw strength from them can be guided to new resources. In reality, much of our Christian pilgrimage is about learning to let go of one way of expressing our faith and trusting the Holy Spirit to lead us to another that will become just as full of life for us.

The daily worship in the classroom at my prep school gave way to worship in a far grander building at my public school. In the era in which I grew up, it seems that children generally went to the school determined for them by parents, and in my case it was always assumed that I would attend the public school that my father and uncle had attended in the 1920s. I am convinced that if I had had any say in the matter, this school would not have been my choice, and, as we drove up to the austere Victorian Gothic buildings of Charterhouse School on a clear September day, some of my worst fears were confirmed. For me, it held nothing but terror in those early days, and the only place of solace and solitude was in the safe confines of the outside toilets, where I would read letters from home that kept me connected with a far warmer and more welcoming world. Quite why the homesickness was so severe, I have never really discovered, but in time its severity passed and I settled.

I don't remember praying in those rather dark days, and there was no great comfort in the vast and lofty Memorial Chapel designed by Sir Giles Gilbert Scott, which was the largest World War I memorial in England. The names of all those dead heroes meant little to me as I wandered through the huge oak doors and sat in the front row with the other new boys amid unwelcome smells of sour wood polish, pubescent sweat and flatulence. In time, however, even this cavernous building became a place of safety for me, and I had my first experiences of being moved, sometimes almost to tears (if I had dared show them), by some of the hymns. Even now, if I hear the powerful setting of George Herbert's poem 'Come, my Way, my Truth, my Life' by Alexander Brent Smith, I feel something of the stirring I felt as we sang the great crescendo at the end of each verse. But generally, in those early days, there was little movement in my spiritual life through the chapel.

The chaplain was a man called Henry Bettenson, who was renowned (so I discovered many years later) as a leading expert on the early Church Fathers. To me he was an elderly man in a black robe with long silver hair, and I imagined that if ever I were to meet such Old Testament prophets as Jeremiah or Ezekiel, that was how they would look. When he prepared a small group of us for confirmation, we met in the huge living-room of his home. We sat in a row beneath a lofty upper gallery, and he explained the faith while walking up and down before us. He spent the entire hour working away at his pipe, digging out old bits of worn-out tobacco and then packing in crumbling, beautiful-smelling tobacco, before combusting the thing with astonishing smoke and drama. I learned nothing about the Christian faith in those sessions but I have never lost my love of the fragrance of pipe-smoke!

It was Bishop George Reindorp who came to confirm us in late November, when hope was rising for the end of term and the Christmas holiday. I was 15 by then, and I remember some boys discussing how the confirmation service could be a religious experience. I liked the sound of this, and as the bishop moved along the Communion rail, confirming us, I remember being touched by the use of our Christian names, for it was the usual custom in school to be addressed only by our surnames. So when the bishop placed his large hands on my head and said 'Confirm, O Lord, thy servant *Michael* with thy Holy Spirit', there was something intrinsically consoling and touching about such a senior figure calling me by my Christian name. In those moments I reached up to heaven with every part of my spirit that I could muster, in the hope of getting some kind of religious experience, but, try as I might, I never 'got' anything to speak of. Others claimed they did but, as far as I was concerned, I was passed by.

However, I did gain a silver propelling pencil, made in England by Yard-O-Led and given to me by my parents, who had taken the trouble to have my initials and date of confirmation engraved on it. The same pencil sits on my desk today, and I have still not worked through the yard of lead that is packed away in neat sections within. Picking it up today reconnects me to that autumn day all those years ago, and it reminds me that the experience of feeling a bit left out of spiritual encounters has often been a feature of my journey. I have noticed it especially in charismatic meetings, where others seem to have such deep and special encounters with God, while I have moments of feeling disturbingly untouched, and come to uncomfortable conclusions about why God should have passed me by once again. That, at least, is how my emotions interpret the experience, but when I push beyond those feelings, I discover that God is not one whose presence and blessing can be summoned up to order or be expressed in the same way for every person.

As I reflect on my confirmation experience now, I see that I would have done well to dwell on the surprise and delight I felt on hearing my Christian name at the altar rail. That, I feel sure, was what God wanted to give me at that moment of confirmation—a revelation that he called me by name. Because I was looking for something else—that experience that the other boys spoke of—I failed to acknowledge the very precious experience that God was giving me. It was a very personal message about how, in a world that can often be cold and hostile, there is a God who turns his face towards us in kindness and calls us his friend. This makes me wonder how often we miss the most beautiful gifts from the hand of God because we have held tight to expectations about what they should look like and how they should feel.

It was not until the end of my school days that I found someone who became my first real tutor in Anglican spirituality. When I was 17, my parents moved house again, this time to another village in Buckinghamshire—Weston Turville. The vicar was Stanley Jones, a single man who occupied his huge vicarage with his mother and an unpleasantly smelly dog. Tea at the vicarage was a mixed blessing when his beloved dog was in the room, but I found conversation with Stanley fascinating. He was a very intelligent but very unselfconfident man who seemed to be nervous of many people and things. He was a high churchman who loved the liturgy and sang the choral parts of the service with a strong, clear voice. I had never come across this kind of service before, as all my Anglican experience had been fairly middle-of-the-road. I rather disliked it at first but I warmed very much to Stanley and it wasn't long before I regarded him as a true friend. Because he was so much more 'normal' than any other vicar or chaplain I had met, he was someone I could trust and, to some extent, relate to. We would talk for ages in his vicarage, and then he would take me across to the church where we would kneel in one of the congregational pews.

My memories of those moments always include sunshine beaming in through the coloured windows, and Stanley praying in his formal yet vulnerable way. Yes, it was Anglican comfort again, but something real was happening and I was getting to know someone who truly loved the Anglican Church. As it turned out, it seemed that it was not a church that really loved Stanley, and I was often saddened to see him burdened under pressures from either the congregation or the diocese. He died suddenly and far too early, while I was a curate, and when the bishop stood in the pulpit and declared, 'Today is a day of joy', I could not have agreed less. Technically the bishop was right, and Stanley had entered into the joy of his Lord, but for me it was a grievous loss of a friend and mentor.

For most of us, it is people rather than books, buildings or events that shape our spiritual journey and give it direction. Yes, there can be wonderful spiritual experiences that have a marked influence on us, and I shall write about some of them later in this book. But I have to say that the chief influence on my journey has been observing the way faith is played out in someone's life. I need to see it work in practice: someone has to incarnate faith, in order for it to make sense to me. When I was ordained in my mid-20s, I made a point of writing to all the people I felt had been messengers of God to me on my journey to this important point in my life. I included a note to the old headmaster of my prep school and received such a moving reply that it had me in tears. He must have had days of wondering whether his diligent tutoring of the boys in Christian faith and worship was having any effect at all, and it was clearly a great comfort to him to know that, for at least one of those boys, the experience had been meaningful and significant.

This headmaster, the village church vicar and a few others along the way were the ones who moved me enough to get me to think about faith. In none of those Anglican churches or chapels did my faith really come alive: that happened separately, but by no means independently. It came as a surprise—not to say shock—when I felt God call me to serve him in the Anglican Church. My call came soon after a strong charismatic experience and I was all for offering myself into Pentecostal ministry. But the word of God to me was clear: I had to serve him in the church of my ancestors and my family. It did not feel a comfortable choice, but I believe it was a right one.

The discomfort has never quite left me. I have now served as an Anglican priest for several decades, and yet I can still feel a little out of place in a big clergy meeting. Even when I was installed as an honorary Canon in Derby Cathedral, at a great service on All Saints Day, there was still a part of me that slipped quietly away from the words of the great hymns and prayers, daydreamed and felt just a little out of place. It is perhaps true for all of us who have drawn from several traditions and spiritualities that no one tradition will seem fully like home to us, and this can make us feel disturbed and possibly lonely, but such disturbance can be very healthy. Psalm 139 is one of the best-known Psalms: it starts, 'O Lord, you have searched me and known me', and continues, 'You search out my path and my lying down, and are acquainted with all my ways.' The God we serve is the one who knows us by name and is familiar with all the pathways of our lives. It seems to me that if we try to conform ourselves to fit exactly with one particular tradition, we may be missing some very important pathways in our souls, pathways that are known to God.

It may be that, for some people, all their pathways can be found in the Anglican tradition, and Anglican life feels like an 'exact fit' for them, but I suspect that for most, this will not be the case. The church of which they are members, whether it be Anglican, Methodist, Baptist, New Church or whatever, will not understand *all* the pathways within them. When one such pathway becomes important for us, and it is one that is not accepted in the church of which we are a member, we become a little lonelier and the church feels a little less like home for us. It is quite possible to live in creative tension with this feeling, but for some people the tension becomes too much and they find they have to move somewhere else. For too many, the 'somewhere else' is a churchless life, because they feel that no church understands them, but the church stream that we connect ourselves with can be a source of great strength to us when we are allowed to own and celebrate the different pathways within us. It can be the firm ground and place of safety from which we do our exploring.

Not long ago, I was invited to do some work with a church in Colorado, that beautiful state in the USA that is dominated by the great Rocky Mountains. The church was situated in the northern part of the state, but, before the visit, my wife and I holidayed in the southern part, in the region just north of New Mexico. One day we drove out to the Mesa Verde National Park. There we visited the beautiful ancient cliff dwellings that once belonged to the Puebloan people. 'Mesa Verde' translates as 'green table', and this massive 'green table' stands high in a plain of indescribable vastness. I am used to viewing plains in England but nothing prepared me for the huge size of this one. To stand on that vast 'green table' and look out at land that stretched far, far away to a most distant horizon was almost eerie. At the same time, though, it was strangely and extraordinarily reassuring. Here was good old planet Earth, providing a solid foundation for our lives. Here we could see a world without too many obvious demands. I suppose you could say that living down there might seem a little boring—you could drive for hours and never climb any hill to speak of—yet the land was by and large fertile and productive and reliable. Of course, if you live down there, you do get a fabulous view of the Mesa Verde, and you can also admire the great snow-peaked mountains of the Rockies. It is a flat land but a good land, and the surrounding geography inspires you to adventure.

This is *my* experience of the Anglican tradition. I am keen to put 'my' in italics here because I am describing my personal experience of Anglicanism. It has offered me a safe foundation for my explorations. It is the land in which I dwell, and it is the home to which I return. It has not provided me with dramas like high mountains or white waters, but from this plain I have caught sight of distant mountains, and it has given me the desire to travel and has served as an excellent base camp for further exploration. I have also found it to be a generous and open land, so that when I come back from my travels with stories of what I have discovered, it delights to hear about my discoveries and is wonderfully respectful of the different geographies and cultures that I have encountered. I sense we all need to find one tradition that serves us in this way—a spiritual homeland that we know our way around and which acts as a blessed fixed point in our lives. I have no doubt that God does indeed bless such plains as these.

Questions for reflection

- How much do you know about the spirituality of your ancestors? If you don't know much, try to find out a little more. To what extent has their faith shaped and influenced yours?
- If you grew up in a churchgoing home, what are your reflections on the Christian tradition that was presented to you? What aspects of it are true to your journey now, and what have you

needed to leave behind? Are there aspects that you need to either let go or rediscover? If you did not grow up in a churchgoing home, what did influence you spiritually as a child?

O Lord, you have searched me out and you know all the pathways of my life. Thank you for the solid plains that have been a homeland to me. When I dwell in these plains, help me to draw from their goodness but also keep my eyes open to the adventures beyond.

Chapter 3

Evangelical home counties

The 'home counties' is a term that has been used since the 19th century to describe the counties surrounding the City of London. I presume it came into use when London became a mighty capital city and its influence stretched throughout the world. It was a kind of epicentre and the neighbouring counties were, in that sense, close to home. Living as I now do in the Midlands, I find, not surprisingly, some resistance to any lingering notion that everything important happens in London. In my teenage years, however, I lived and went to school in the home counties and some of my family still live there.

When I drive down to Buckinghamshire, I am driving away from my home county of Derbyshire to an old 'home county', for which I still have great affection and where I have a sense of belonging. Any who find themselves now living in a part of the country different from where they grew up will experience that original region as something like a 'home county', with strong resonances of belonging about it.

As we trace our spiritual journey, we may find a similar kind of relationship with a spiritual tradition that has something of the feel of a 'home county' about it. It is the tradition that played a major part in bringing us to life spiritually and nurturing us. It is where faith came alive, God became real and we made important decisions about believing in Christ and following him. Some people settle into their 'home county' tradition and remain quite happily there for the rest of their lives. Others can, over time, develop quite a sharp reaction against it for all kinds of reasons and abandon it in favour of another land that feels far more like home. Yet others, like myself, still view it with gratitude and affection but recognise that it has not been our only land of habitation.

In my early teenage years I stumbled across a society at school that was called 'The Christian Union'. That was its official title but it was known to most as 'God Soc' and was viewed by almost all the other boys in my school with grave suspicion and some disdain. Quite how I ventured into my first meeting, I'm not quite sure, but one way or another I made my way through the mockery of fellow pupils and turned up one Sunday afternoon to one of the meetings. Almost immediately I was aware of two conflicting feelings: the first was a sense that if there was any place on earth where faith in God was alive, real and relevant, it was here. Something in the teachers and boys who attended assured me that their faith meant something and did something. The conflicting feeling was to do with the culture: something about the way they talked and behaved did not feel quite 'me'. Thankfully, though, my curiosity was stronger than my anxiety (an important battle to be won in any spiritual exploration) and after a time I became a regular attender.

The meetings were led by two teachers, Cary Gilbart-Smith and Graham Leask. In time, I came to regard these two teachers with enormous respect as I watched them withstand the fierce onslaught of 1960s secularism and ridicule and meet it with truly impressive gentleness and grace.

In my first summer term, the Christian Union organised a coach trip to London to hear the renowned American evangelist, Billy Graham. I had never heard of him but I liked the idea of a free coach trip to London and so did many of my friends. Thus it was, in the summer of 1967, that I found myself making my way into the huge auditorium of Earls Court and, armed with Coke, sweets and crisps, settled down to listen to what the man had to say. I was on the point of assuming my usual 'church leaders are boring so what shall I think about today?' mode when Billy Graham started his address, and for the first time in my life I was utterly captivated by a religious speaker. He spoke as one who really did believe all this stuff about Jesus. Not only did he believe it but it made a profound difference to the way he lived and behaved and treated others. He seemed more alive than any preacher I had come across hitherto. Unlike the preachers in my home church and school chapel, this man actually connected with my world and used God-language that I could understand. More than that, he spoke with an authority that I had not witnessed before, so much so that when he said, 'I want you to come out of your seats and come down here and give your lives to Christ,' there was little argument about it in my mind.

I have often thought about that moment and wondered whether I was an impressionable teenager at the mercy of some kind of manipulation, but in all honesty I do not think that was the case for me. I was at a place of openness in my spiritual journey. I just needed someone to speak sense to me, a bit like the Ethiopian eunuch in Acts 8:26–40. I was far from being an important foreign dignitary riding in my chariot, but, like that Ethiopian, I had developed questions about God. What I heard in church, school chapel and even Christian Union made little sense to me and did not seem to be relevant to my life. Something about the American preacher was relevant, and when I heard the good news from him, I did the equivalent of getting out of my chariot and coming close to those who could guide me.

Once down in the main auditorium, with the massed choir singing 'Just as I am without one plea', I was ushered to a man called Philip who, despite his nervousness, did a wonderful job of reassuring me and explaining what it meant to follow Jesus. He was one of those whom I wrote to when I was ordained, and his letter back to me is also one that I treasure. Thus I returned triumphantly to school and proclaimed that I was 'converted', and the weeks that followed remain the only time in my life when I would say that I encountered something like persecution. It was, of course, nothing like the terrible persecutions that Christians have suffered in very hostile communities, but it was sharp enough for me and I was still struggling with insecurities and homesickness. Nonetheless, I wasn't going to give up the faith that had been such a delight to discover. It felt as if God had shifted out of the rafters of the church and chapel, down to my level, and was now involving himself in my life. Mine was a very infant faith, but it was not a bad start at all.

However, the long school holidays followed, without the support of the Christian Union, and when I went back to school I slipped out of the habit of attending their meetings. As I mentioned in the last chapter, I was confirmed, and, in longing for one expression of the presence of God, I missed his personal word to me. However, the leaders of the Christian Union would not forget me, and Christian friends kept a look-out for me. The two teachers were terribly keen to get me to go to Iwerne Minster. This was a summer houseparty that took place in a prep school on the south coast. The events were also affectionately known as 'Bash Camps' after the founder and leader, E.J.H. Nash (known by all as 'Bash'). The thought of spending a week of my precious holidays in a school environment was quite anathema to me. When I discovered that these holidays were terribly sporty as well, I dug my heels in even further. Nevertheless, somehow I was persuaded to go one summer and I loathed it as much as I'd thought I would. Again, it was something about the sheer male heartiness of the culture that put me off, although I will say that some of the evening talks were magnificent and I know my spirit was touched in those moments.

Thankfully, there was a less hearty version of the camps on offer over New Year, held at what was then called the Oxford Polytechnic, now Oxford Brookes University. It was at this houseparty in the New Year of 1969/70 that something clicked again for me. David MacInnes (who later became the vicar of St Aldates, Oxford) was the speaker and, like Billy Graham, he spoke with clarity and conviction and I found his message and his exposition of the scriptures full of life and wisdom. I think, at this stage, my faith was more intellectual than emotional. David MacInnes and the other speakers present gave me good reason to believe in Jesus and to follow him, and I remember being aware that this was the point in my life when I would make a very serious decision. I would either believe that the Jesus written about in the scriptures was alive or I would give up the whole thing as rubbish. I had to choose: I could not dither for the rest of my life. I could leave that conference confidently as a Christian, or I could decide that Jesus was not alive, go away and live my life without him and find some other set of beliefs to follow.

It did not take me long to decide: I chose to follow Jesus, and the context of this choice was the conservative evangelical tradition. I went home and told friends that I had become a Christian. I was born again. I was saved. I had given my life to Jesus. All this terminology now rolled off my tongue fairly naturally (never *fully* naturally). As far as the Christian Union was concerned, I was 'soundly converted', I had 'come right through' and I was 'on great form'. As I reflect on these experiences, I do so with a huge sense of gratitude. It was just what I needed at this stage in my life, and I doubt that any other tradition would have done it for me. I cringe now at some of the language I used and how uncritically I fell into the culture of that spirituality, but I do know that it gave me the clarity and confidence I needed at the time.

Perhaps, in the plans of God for us, he does steer us towards particular traditions at particular seasons of our lives, because it is through those traditions that we can hear his voice in the way we need to. Over the years I have met many people who have come to faith by a completely different route and through a very different tradition. I have met those who wandered into very sacramental churches and found themselves caught up in a sense of the holiness and presence of God, such that faith rose up in them and they made a decision to follow Christ. No sermons, no 'get up out of your seats', no booklets about the cross and the Four Spiritual Laws—just a life-changing encounter. For others, their journey to faith has come through rubbing shoulders with Christians who were working on the edges of society and demonstrating the compassion of Jesus so wonderfully that they simply couldn't fail to be drawn to him.

Evangelicalism was my way into faith and there is much in this tradition that I still value and cherish. It has undoubtedly shaped my Christian life. The word 'evangelical' comes from the Greek word for gospel (*evangelion*). At the heart of evangelicalism is a passion to believe the gospel and spread the gospel, and see people converted to Christ. The term came into currency in church life during the 18th century, particularly with the development of Pietism in Germany and the Netherlands, and then through the ministry of the Wesleys in Britain and America. Evangelists such as Jonathan Edwards were hugely influential in the USA.

Evangelicalism flourished in the 19th century with the great expansion of missionary work and its keen concern for social reform. William Wilberforce was perhaps the greatest example of an evangelical, whose faith drove him to fight relentlessly against the horrors of slavery (which was, disturbingly, supported by many in the church at the time). The 19th century also saw the emergence of great evangelical preachers such as Charles Spurgeon and Dwight L. Moody. A more doctrinally conscious evangelicalism developed in reaction to Darwin and proponents of Enlightenment thinking, and evangelical fundamentalism emerged as a kind of counterbalance to the unnerving secularism that was influencing so many at the time. This fundamentalism grew strong in the 20th century, fuelled in some places by association with Pentecostalism. Critics of evangelicalism often cite stories from fundamentalist evangelicals, which is very unfair as vast numbers of evangelicals would be just as critical of fundamentalism as anyone else.

This is where it gets complicated, because 21st-century evangelicalism is actually a mixture of traditions. My own journey is typical of a road that many have travelled in recent years. Following my New Year houseparty experience, I had no trouble in calling myself an evangelical. I discovered that it was possible to be an evangelical without having to be hearty and sporty. I could, generally speaking, be myself. As a young Christian, I did not mind being dependent on Christian leaders to guide me (all leaders were men in those days), so I would listen avidly to Christian Union speakers and take lots of notes. I would read books by authors such as John Stott and I discovered a deep love for the Bible. I learned to pray aloud in prayer groups and began to use words like 'fellowship' without embarrassment. When I returned home in the holidays, I mostly kept quiet about it all but wrote lots of letters to evangelical friends. Thankfully, my greatest friend at school, Robert, did not live far from me, and he was on a very similar spiritual journey to my own, so we would meet up and keep our relatively newfound faith alive. The friendship with Robert was enormously helpful to me, as he also had a strong allergic reaction to the heartiness of the Bash Camps; he was wonderfully human, which meant that he kept me from becoming unbearably pious in my evangelicalism.

In those days I lived in two Christian worlds—the evangelical world of the Christian Union and the Anglican world of chapel and church—and although this meant that I had something of a split personality, generally speaking I was happy with it and could make it work.

In my last couple of years at school, a Welshman called John Peters came to the school and became one of my A Level English teachers. We soon discovered that he too was evangelical (a very rare breed among the teachers), though of a rather different type, not least in that he was not Anglican. We discovered that he went to a Plymouth Brethren church, and, as we used to holiday in Devon as a child, I instinctively liked the sound of it. In my naivety I knew of very few denominations other than the Anglican and Catholic churches, so to discover a new one was really quite exciting.

One day John took me and another friend, called Gerald, to his church. I was surprised by how different it was, architecturally, from the Anglican churches I knew. It was a small, low-ceilinged building with chairs, not pews, and absolutely no religious furniture that I could recognise. It could have been a classroom, although it was much more welcoming than the classrooms of our school. The atmosphere was pleasant and the hymn singing very stirring, despite the fact that I knew none of the hymns.

Gerald and I attended several of these services with our teacher, and what we particularly liked was the informality. There was no liturgy, so we were spared the sense that I experienced so often in school chapel of hearing words being spoken but not meant. Lots of people stood up and shared thoughts from the Bible, they prayed out loud, and when someone prayed, everyone else seemed to join in with 'Mmm's and 'Yes, Lord's and other signs that they hadn't fallen asleep but were actually participating. Although it was all a little chummier than I would have liked, it was generally a very positive experience. It was a church full of people who really believed, and believed in such a way that it clearly affected the way they lived. Here I witnessed a Christian community who met together on a Sunday, and what happened among them when they met made a big difference to the way they lived through the week.

It is perhaps helpful to reflect on the tradition in which our faith came alive for us and, as far as possible, to feel our way back into those early experiences. Often, with the passing of time, we can judge the past rather harshly, particularly if we feel in some way embarrassed by our naiveties and inexperience. But the fact is that, for us at that particular stage of our lives, it was important. It was the nursery for our faith, and the things we loved about that particular tradition were valuable to us, even if we came to ask questions of that nursery later in life. It is worth looking back and asking, 'Why was I drawn to this?' As I write, I realise that, for me, it was necessary to find an expression of faith that had some life about it. I was living, to some extent, in reaction to my experience of Anglicanism, which had been very formal, rigid and unconnected with the everyday world. Billy Graham, the Christian Union and these Plymouth Brethren believers all clearly loved Jesus from the bottom of their hearts. Their emotions were involved, even though they were careful about showing them in public. They clearly *felt* their faith, and it shaped the way they lived. I was looking for a spirituality in which following Jesus touched my feelings, and which changed how I lived, how I viewed the world and how I treated others.

I also loved the way the Bible came alive in the evangelical meetings I attended. The Bible wasn't just a textbook; it was a book that people loved. Old evangelicals came to meetings carrying huge black Bibles with torn covers; every page had wide margins which were covered in notes in tiny handwriting. I bought myself one such Bible and immediately set to work writing my notes in the margins. The Bible wasn't just a book full of meaning, but it was a book that in itself was loved. I know some critics of evangelicalism talk about 'bibliolatry' (worshipping the Bible), but in my experience I have never witnessed it. I have always observed a lovely reverence for the Bible and great conviction that, as the written word of God, it merits great respect. In later years, of course, I discovered that evangelicals were greatly divided about the interpretation of many of the texts, but in those early days, that love for the Bible was very special for me. Every day I would pore over my Revised Standard Version, and it really did feel as if the scriptures I read were a personal word from God to me. I have never lost this conviction. Even now, as I pick up my Bible, I feel the same love and I have the same expectation that any word I read could be a personal word from God to me, to sustain me on my journey through the day.

The older I get, the more I realise that I will never learn all the wisdom there is to learn from the scriptures, because one lifetime is just not enough. I am very much aware that the Bible has been used in all kinds of unhealthy and manipulative ways by Christians of all traditions, but perhaps especially by evangelicals. I have never had much patience with arguments about what the 'inerrancy' of scripture means, and whether stories such as the Adam and Eve narratives are fact or parable. For me, this misses the point—but I think I am now straying into the chapter on the liberal tradition! At this stage, I am acknowledging the debt I owe to the evangelical tradition for giving me a love for the scriptures: it is one that I know I will never lose.

I am also grateful for the emphasis placed by evangelicalism on personal faith and the expectation that we will talk naturally about that faith to others. The Christianity in which I was raised believed that faith was a private affair, not for wider discussion. Evangelicalism taught me that my faith is worth sharing. I have to admit that I never find it easy to approach a stranger and launch into a conversation about God: I still find it quite hard to get going on the subject even with the people I know. However, I believe it is important for faith to reside so naturally in our lives that when the moment arises, we find it as easy to talk about as the weather. Some other traditions view this easygoing approach with some awkwardness, but personal evangelism remains a very strong feature of evangelicalism.

My final year or two at school were happy by and large, though overshadowed by abysmal A Level results. I was mentally paralysed by fear throughout most of them and the results showed it. By now I had received my call to ordained ministry, and my preferred route for training was to go to university to study for a degree in theology. If I had gained good grades in my A Levels, I might have had some choice about which university to attend. However, beggars can't be choosers, and I ended up happy to go to any university that would have me. It turned out that the university that decided to risk giving me a place was Exeter, in my much-beloved county of Devon, home county of my grandmother and the location of many happy family holidays.

My happiness over gaining a place at Exeter was tempered just a little by a letter I received a couple of months later from one of the prominent leaders of the Bash Camps, who wrote strongly advising me to turn down the place. His reason was that Exeter was renowned as the most liberal faculty in the country, and a three-year exposure to such an environment could apparently do untold damage to my faith. I had been identified as a promising young evangelical leader who could be lost in such a hostile environment. The evangelicals of the Bash Camps already had concerns for me because of my dalliance with Pentecostalism (the subject of the next chapter). To them, the combination of Pentecostalism and liberalism was a toxic mix.

I remember being particularly annoyed by the letter, because it felt as if someone was trying to control me. Although this control was being expressed with signs of respect and affection, it still felt quite threatening. I was having to face the rather disturbing truth that the expression of Christianity I had seen in my school Christian Union and the Plymouth Brethren was beginning to look limited. I was starting to feel cramped. I had got far enough into this tradition to gain quite a strong sense of belonging; I had learned the language and was 'part of the club', but the leaders of that club were seriously concerned for me and I keenly felt their disapproval. This brings into play a difficult aspect of all spiritual traditions, which is the disturbing existence of party loyalty.

Within human nature there is an instinctive tribalism: we yearn to be part of a group of people, wider than our family, where we feel a keen sense of belonging. Humans all too easily develop strong personal loyalties to a particular tribe, and the emotional and social investment in that tribe is high. Go to any football match and you will witness it; if you are a supporter of one of the teams, note your passionate feelings for your side and your antipathy towards the other. If a member of your team is accused of a foul, you will probably disagree with the referee, but if the opposition is accused, you will think, 'Good judgment, Ref!' Take this principle to the far grimmer stage of inter-tribal tension that we have seen in parts of Africa, and we become all too aware of how tribal loyalty can lead to dreadful acts of violence. Christianity has not avoided such violence, as we have seen in the sad story of the Troubles in Northern Ireland.

Tribal loyalty is an instinct that lies deep in the human soul. Thus, in our journey of faith, when we discover a sense of belonging to a particular tradition of the church, tribal instincts can be stirred. I became aware of this when I received that well-meaning letter from the camp leader, and I remember taking a clear decision that I never wanted to 'belong' to one single church tradition. To me, it spoke of a world where I would have to surrender my power to think for myself and hand it over to others more learned, more biblical, more 'sound' than I. I was keen to find out things for myself and trust God to lead me. This is not to say that I despised the guidance of older and wiser believers. It was simply that I didn't want to be trapped in a world of party loyalties.

I have no doubt that many who make a journey into just one tradition of the church do so because there is such a close harmony between who they are and the values of that tradition that it is a very good 'fit'. However, I fear that there are others who remain part of a particular tradition because they dare not leave. They know it would hurt and upset people who are very dear to them. It would be like a 'coming out' to friends and family—and let no one underestimate how hard such an experience can be and what risks are involved.

A relatively recent development in evangelical thinking is called 'post-evangelicalism'. The term initially found currency in the mid-1990s and was the title of a provocative book by Dave Tomlinson, a former New Church leader and now an Anglican minister. Within a decade, it was in popular use in the UK and USA and, very generally speaking, it is now applied to people who once found a home in evangelicalism but discovered it to be restrictive in terms of theology, culture and spirituality. Some wanted to break away and gain some independence but did not want to cut off all ties with the original tribe. Not surprisingly, some in the original tribe took great exception to the post-evangelicals' watering down (as they saw it) of some of their important beliefs and customs. As a result, there has been some tribal tension, and while there is no doubting the existence of the new tribe of post-evangelicals, it is probably truer to describe it as a collection of micro-tribes.

If such a concept had existed in the early 1970s, I guess I would quickly have become post-evangelical. As it was, I remained in the evangelical tribe, journeyed on to Exeter University and settled into studying its liberal theology. My evangelicalism was kept alive by close association with the university Christian Union. It is probably true to say, however, that I was kept in the CU not so much by the evangelical life as by the charismatic renewal that was gusting through the university at the time.

Even a cursory reading of the Gospels reveals that Jesus had no real fondness for tribalism of any kind. The sharpest expressions of tribalism in his day were the sects of the Pharisees, Sadducees, Zealots and Essenes. The two mentioned most often are the Pharisees and Sadducees, and Jesus had precious little good to say about either of them. In Matthew 23, where we read of Jesus 'seven woes' directed at the Pharisees and teachers of the law, he accuses the Pharisees of shutting the door of the kingdom of heaven in people's faces (v. 13) by laying impossible religious burdens on them. While it would be unfair to compare any Christian tradition to the Pharisees, there is a warning here for the leaders of any Christian group to guard against the dangers of seeking to control its members. Jesus wanted people to be free (John 8:36), and that freedom included allowing them to think for themselves. This is why he taught so often in parables: he was not telling people what to believe and how to behave, but encouraging them to come to their own conclusions.

In my experience of 'conservative evangelicalism' (as it is sometimes called today), it felt quite controlling, and I was looking for something in which I could do more thinking for myself. What I discovered was that there was another type of evangelicalism that I had found neither in the Bash Camps nor in the Plymouth Brethren. It was a charismatic evangelicalism, which was, for me, a pathway of freedom. This will be the subject of the next chapter.

Questions for reflection

- What is your 'home county'? What aspects of it helped you come alive in your faith? How do you feel about it today?
- As you think about your tradition, do you detect any danger that it might be 'tribal' in the way I have described in this chapter? Do you ever feel disloyal when you explore other traditions? What do you think God feels about any such disloyalty?

Thank you, Father, for those who led me to faith and for the 'home counties' where that faith was nurtured. Please lead me to journey in such a way that my faith stays alive and growing and brings life to those whom I meet on the road.

Chapter 4

Charismatic streams

The spirituality of about a quarter of all Christians in the world goes back to a most unlikely event at the beginning of the 20th century. In the final years of the 19th century there had been a growing conviction among some North American Christians that they should pray for the 'latter rain' of revival, as prophesied by the prophet Joel (2:23), and that this would be the prelude to the second coming of Jesus. In April 1906, in a tiny mission church in Los Angeles, something happened that many came to regard as the answer to their prayer, and the leader of this movement was a black preacher called William Seymour.

William was born in 1870 of parents who were former slaves in Louisiana. While he attended a church in Houston, he was immensely moved by a woman called Lucy Farrow, who spoke in a prayer language that he had never before witnessed, and it engendered in him an intense spiritual longing. Lucy introduced William to a man called Charles Fox Parham, for whom she had once worked as a governess. He now ran the Bethel Bible College, and William was keen to join it. There was only one problem: Parham was a Klu Klux Klan sympathiser and so had great misgivings about allowing a black man to enter his college. Yet he did not want to appear uncharitable, so he allowed William to listen to the college lectures while seated on a chair outside an open window.

William was not put off by such inhospitality; he soaked up the teaching and found himself longing for the 'baptism of the

Holy Spirit' and the gift of tongues. He became a preacher initially in Houston and later in Los Angeles, where a certain Sister Julia Hutchins had rented a storefront on Santa Fe Avenue and invited him to be the preacher there. After a short time, she found that she did not care for his theology, so William ministered on his own, gathering a group of black domestic servants and washerwomen. In one of the prayer meetings, William Seymour was suddenly given the gift of tongues for which he had so earnestly prayed, and his preaching caught fire. Crowds started to gather, so he rented a vacant two-storey building at 312 Azusa Street, which had been a church, a warehouse and most recently a stable. The rest, as they say, is history. From this tiny beginning, a worldwide revival transformed the shape of the church in the 20th century.[4]

For half of the century, this vigorous and fast-growing movement drew people into a powerful experience of the Holy Spirit and enabled them to use gifts of the Spirit detailed in 1 Corinthians 12, such as speaking in tongues, healing and prophecy. It had a strong missional component, so the spiritual fire spread fast all over the world. Generally speaking, it did not make great headway in the denominational churches until the second half of the century. When, on 3 April 1960, the Revd Dennis Bennett, Rector of St Mark's Episcopal Church in Van Nuys, California, announced from his pulpit during the parish Eucharist that he been baptised in the Holy Spirit and spoke in tongues, the shockwaves reverberated around the Anglican communion and he quickly became something of a celebrity. Here was a perfectly normal, decent Anglican doing something that only wild Pentecostals did.

It wasn't long before Anglicans in Britain started to be affected, the most notable being a young curate called Michael Harper who was serving with the well-established evangelical vicar of All Souls Langham Place, John Stott. Not long after his experience, Michael set up the Fountain Trust, which became an ecumenical channel of Pentecostal experience for those in the denominational churches. This fast-flowing stream of Pentecostal life became known as 'the charismatic movement', and its influence spread rapidly across the country, even reaching a couple of young evangelical pupils in their final year at Charterhouse School in Surrey.

Due to my lamentable A Level results, I had remained at school with a view to retaking my exams. As it happened, my unexpected acceptance as a theology undergraduate at Exeter University meant that re-sits were unnecessary, but, rather than leaving school, I embarked on an excellent pre-university course that the school ran, which turned out to be probably the best term's education I had experienced. By now we were into the 1970s and many of the old school rules had been relaxed; as a senior boy I also had new freedoms which included not always having to go to chapel on Sundays. Hence my good friend Gerald and I were able to visit the Plymouth Brethren church instead.

In our discussions, Gerald and I found ourselves increasingly dissatisfied with all of the traditions of Christianity that we had so far discovered—Anglican, CU and Brethren. There was an indefinable something for which we yearned intensely, and we prayed to God for it. The school chaplain at this time was a very genial liberal churchman, who had been joined by a colleague called Bill Aitken. Bill was primarily a maths teacher in the school but, as he was ordained, served also as a part-time chaplain. He had just returned from missionary work in war-torn Biafra and brought stories of revival with him that troubled the chaplain and excited us.

Gerald returned from the Christmas holidays clutching a book that he had picked up from his local Anglican church in Kent. It was by Michael Harper, leader of the Fountain Trust, and it was called *Power for the Body of Christ*. We both read the book avidly and it filled us with excitement. Michael's careful evangelical teaching suited us and it provided clear advice on how to receive the Spirit in the charismatic way. We asked the chaplain if we could use his vestry for prayer meetings and he duly agreed, little imagining that a couple of boys were seeking a charismatic experience. We prayed and prayed but nothing happened, so we decided we had to look for help. If God wanted us baptised in the Holy Spirit, we would have to go and collect it from a church that could deliver it. We skipped chapel one cold February Sunday morning, hopped on a train to Guildford and walked out of the station praying, 'Lord, if you want this to happen to us, lead us to a church that will do it.' Thus we found ourselves wandering around the back streets of Guildford, looking for churches and finding nothing until we came to a tiny tin-roofed building with a broken noticeboard, one word on which was still legible: 'Elim'. The word meant nothing to me but to Gerald it was a clue. He remembered that at the prayer meeting at his local church in Kent, they sang from a songbook that was something to do with Elim. That was enough for us!

We entered the church and were warmly welcomed by the pastor, who showed us to seats near the back of the church. Anxiety now started to rise in me as I wondered what I had let myself in for. Had I landed myself among the most deranged Christians in the world? And would I have to hang on for dear life while ecstatic people roared in tongues around me? We had also heard (I can't imagine from where) that levitation was not uncommon in Pentecostal churches. Worst of all, would Gerald and I end up being hopelessly conspicuous as those most clearly *not* baptised in the Spirit, and therefore deemed unspiritual and unsaved?

Sometimes we find ourselves moving into new spiritual traditions almost by chance, while at other times we yearn for something new, and the yearning has to be matched by a willingness to explore and take risks. I was most certainly in the second category and found myself feeling very vulnerable at the start of the service, but I think, in retrospect, such vulnerability also created a sense of openness. I had to demonstrate—if not to God, then certainly to myself—that I was serious about my quest. I would push out into uncomfortable life experiences in order to find what I was searching for. I was prepared to leave my comfort zones and risk loneliness, ridicule, disappointment—whatever it might cost—in order to find the thing for which my spirit was yearning. I knew that I longed to encounter God at a deeper and more powerful level. There had to be more to Christianity than what I had hitherto experienced, and I was prepared to search high and low for it.

Of all the traditions that have been part of my Christian life, the charismatic tradition is the one that felt most risky to encounter, and I think I am not alone in feeling that way. Ever since it first came on the scene, Christians, particularly from the denominational churches, have been anxious about the level of emotion that they see at the meetings. To many, it seems full of dangers—emotionalism, manipulation and hysteria, to name but a few. Yet I thank God that from somewhere I found the courage to be sitting in that cold chapel, nervously wondering what was going to happen next.

As it turned out, what actually happened was not too different from the Brethren services we had attended. I did experience a moment of great alarm when, right at the start of the service, the pastor announced, 'We shall sing hymn 458 and we shall leave our seats in verse 3.' My fears were such that I was convinced the congregation would embark on mass levitation at this point. I was relieved to discover that we were simply required to stand up. What was new for me was the speaking in tongues, but in a way it was not very strange, for it only sounded like someone speaking in a foreign language, and no one appeared to do anything too peculiar in response to it. Also, one gentleman spoke a 'scripture' that I did not recognise, and I later discovered that it was a prophecy delivered in immaculate King James Bible English.

After the service, we went to the pastor and enquired whether he did baptism in the Holy Spirit and, if so, could he give it to us now? I think he was a little surprised by the request, but when the congregation had dispersed, he led us to the 'upper room' (which we acknowledged to be appropriate and biblical!) and he and another elder laid hands on us both.

I don't think I will ever be able adequately to explain what happened to me that morning. Only once before had a religious leader laid hands on me, and that was the Bishop of Guildford at my rather disappointing confirmation service. Now the laying on of hands felt completely different. For a start, the freezing room immediately changed temperature. How you might explain this, I don't know, but from shivering with cold, I started to perspire with the heat. I then found a language bubbling up from inside me, and out it came as speaking in tongues. The curious thing about it was that it did not feel as if I had discovered a new language, more that I had at last found *my* language and it felt wonderfully normal and releasing. It was as if an underground stream had suddenly broken through the earth and could at last flow free. So there we were, two public school boys in the upper room of a downtown Pentecostal church on a cold February morning, receiving fire from heaven that was to change our lives.

Neither of us had ever known anything like this, and we staggered away from the building unsure quite what to do next. We made our way to Guildford high street and, by this time, astonishment had been replaced by helpless laughter. We could hardly walk for it, and it became imperative not to look at one another, for if we did we would become quite unable to move any further. We made our way into the local Wimpy bar, and, despite trying our very best to control ourselves, our order to the waitress was virtually nonsensical. Eventually she understood us, and then, with a very concerned look on her face, asked, 'Have you been drinking?' We knew enough about the Acts 2 story to realise that something truly authentic had been taking place!

We went to the Christian Union that afternoon and told the others all about it. The cool reception from the CU teachers took us by surprise. We then told our Plymouth Brethren teacher and he looked hard at us and said, 'That is the work of the devil. You must keep well clear of it.' Nothing on earth could persuade me that my experience had anything to do with the devil: I felt so full of the light and love of God that such an indictment failed to disturb me. The school chaplain soon got wind of it and said to Bill Aitken, his missionary colleague, 'A terrible thing has happened—Michael and Gerald have been baptised in the Spirit. This must be stopped', to which Bill, with his experience of revival in Biafra, apparently replied, 'You are a mighty man if you can stop the Holy Spirit!'

I can't deny it was disappointing to discover that the two spiritualities that had been so important to me, Anglican and evangelical, regarded my newfound spiritual freedom with such suspicion. After a few weeks, the great Bash unexpectedly turned up to the Christian Union one Sunday, and Gerald and I were invited to have tea with him. As Bash dropped a sugar cube into his cup of Earl Grey tea, he looked searchingly at us and said, 'I can see you have been particularly blessed recently.' I have to confess that neither Gerald nor I gave anything away that afternoon. We changed the subject, talking of the weather and cricket as we sipped our tea, and poor Bash looked disappointed and troubled. We both sensed that there would be no negotiation, no real respect for our experience. It would all be about putting us right, and we were in no mood for it.

At first I assumed that the only way forward for me was to depart from the Anglican and evangelical traditions, and I felt a little sad at the thought of leaving the churches and their spirituality behind. By this stage I had been feeling a strong call to ordained ministry but, given the response I had received from the school chaplain and the CU, I quickly assumed that I would no longer be welcome, and that my task now was to set about offering myself to the Pentecostal Church. Curiously, though, two weeks after the event, I had an overwhelming conviction that I had to be ordained into the Anglican Church. It came as an absolute certainty, completely surprising me and making little sense at the time. I knew I must offer myself to the Church of England but harboured a strong sense that I would not be accepted, especially as I was tainted with all this Pentecostal business.

I was learning an early lesson that moving into another tradition does not mean abandoning the previous one. It was quite possible to be Anglican, evangelical and Pentecostal all together. Nowadays we are very familiar with evangelical charismatic Anglicanism—much of the New Wine movement is exactly that—but in the early 1970s the combination was rare. The mixture of those three traditions made me worry that there would be very few places on earth where I might find a place of belonging. All the Anglican churches I knew were traditional or high church and were suspicious of evangelical and charismatic life; the evangelicals I knew distanced themselves from me because I was now charismatic and going to a liberal theological faculty; the Pentecostals I knew had little time for the institutional church, and the strong line in those days was to 'come out' from the old denominations and join the fresh new churches. For a time, then, I had to settle with feeling peculiar and rather alone.

I don't think this is an unfamiliar experience for those who are making the transition to a new spirituality. A new sense of identity develops. You start mixing with people you didn't mix with before, even those of whom you were rather suspicious. You have to manage the sense of betrayal that you feel when those to whom you once felt so close now seem more distant and appear to be looking anxiously at you.

By this stage of my life, the charismatic experience was the most important for me, and so, when I went to Exeter University, I joined a new 'house church' that was growing fast. After a while, though, I also felt a need for some Anglican life. A few of us drifted into a fairly traditional church in the city centre, and I found that I was well able to live in these two worlds. I still had not found a mix of Anglican, evangelical and charismatic—but then I discovered the Fountain Trust.

Michael Harper had founded and now led the Fountain Trust and, in the early 1970s, he set up a number of international and ecumenical conferences for people to learn about and experience the charismatic renewal. I attended the 1974 conference, held at Nottingham University. For me, it was like entering heaven! All dimensions of my Christian experience found some expression at this conference. Many of the leaders were Anglicans; many were evangelical, including David MacInnes, who had been such an influence on me at that important New Year conference. The theological seminars connected with my interest in theology, which was developing through my studies at Exeter University.

There were also new insights and experiences. One of the main speakers was an Episcopalian priest, Graham Pulkingham. He brought a whole new understanding of community, which involved his Houston church in expressing a remarkable depth of care for the poor of their city, where miracles were interwoven with costly acts of compassion. He brought with him a worship group called the Fisherfolk, which, in time, became very influential in the renewal movement. Through this group, I experienced worship that engaged my emotions in ways I did not think were possible, and it was during a time of worship led by the Fisherfolk that I suddenly discovered myself singing a hymn with my hands raised high in the air. They also brought in the arts, including dance, and they used liturgy in imaginative ways. This combination of worshipping with feeling and imagination, discovering a charismatic community that reached with such compassion to the broken members of society, and making a commitment to rigorous theological reflection was a very heady mix, and I never lost my desire to see this holistic dimension to charismatic renewal.

On our journeys, when we find a spirituality that feels particularly important to us, it is not unusual to have occasional experiences in which that spirituality seems to be at its best, and the Nottingham conference was just that for me. Perhaps this was because the movement was still new and fresh, and I'm sure there was a certain amount of idealism in me that coloured my experience, but I have come to recognise that such times should be treasured. Others would have had very different experiences from mine at that conference, and perhaps some would have found it very difficult, but for me it was a precious discovery. I had found a holistic model of charismatic life, and, even as I write now, so many years later, I sense a longing to remain true to the vision of renewal I witnessed there. There is real value in revisiting such experiences and reminding ourselves of what is important to us.

I was so taken by the vision of community expressed at the conference that I decided to spend a year in community myself, after my studies at Exeter. Christian communities were springing up all over the place in the mid-1970s, and many of them floundered as people realised that living with other humans was far from easy. The community I joined was based in the tiny village of Cuddington, Buckinghamshire, and was led by a young couple, John and Ros Harding. I lived as part of their extended family for a year, and it was a deeply happy and fulfilling time. We certainly found that our vulnerabilities were exposed through living together, but we also discovered the richness of the shared life of Christ, and charismatic experience was very much part of the mix.

From this community I journeyed to another—St John's Theological College in Nottingham. This college had taken the bold decision to embrace the charismatic renewal that, by the late 1970s, was starting to have a strong influence on the church. I was delighted to find myself living in a community that so openly encouraged the use of the charismatic gifts and was willing to experiment and theologically reflect on the experiences. Healing was starting to emerge as a strong aspect of charismatic life in Anglican churches and, at St John's, a particular interest developed in inner healing. This was due partly to the fact that Dr Frank Lake (a Christian psychiatrist and founder of the Clinical Theology Association) developed a close association with the college. Charismatic influences were evident in our worship and were discussed in lectures, and many of us met informally in small groups to pray for physical and emotional healing. For me, such meetings led to very significant emotional healing, for which I will always be grateful, and these experiences gave me the strength and inner security to face the barrage of pressures and stresses that assail clergy in their parish ministries.

By the time I was ordained in 1978, many evangelical churches had experienced charismatic renewal and the church where I trained as a curate—St Andrew's, High Wycombe—was very much alive in this dimension when I arrived. I greatly appreciated learning from John Hughes, my training incumbent, how to encourage renewal in an evangelical Anglican church in a way that would positively inspire its life and mission. This meant that when I went to the Worcester Diocese in the early 1980s, to be the Team Vicar of St Chad's Church, Kidderminster, I had some expertise in leading a church in renewal.

By now, the national Fountain Trust organisation had disbanded and an enterprising vicar from Yorkshire, Lawrence Hoyle, founded Anglican Renewal Ministries, an organisation devoted to encouraging charismatic life in the Anglican church. Early on in my time in Kidderminster, I met one or two other charismatic clergy and we decided to approach the bishop to see if he would allow us to start a Diocesan Renewal Group. He agreed, and one of our first events was to hold a diocesan Eucharist at which the bishop presided and David MacInnes was the guest preacher. We hoped for about 200 people to come and were astonished to find that the cathedral was filled with over 900. We also invited Lawrence Hoyle to lead a teaching day at the Bishop's House for clergy and leaders, which again proved very successful.

The same Lawrence Hoyle, when his doctor advised him to take early retirement, listened to God as to who should succeed him as Director of Anglican Renewal Ministries, and, in doing so, believed that he heard my name. Thus it was, after many doubts, explorations, interviews and confirming signs, that my family and I drove away with much sadness from the parish we loved, to embark on a very new line of work as I became Lawrence's successor.

I spent eight years working as Director of Anglican Renewal Ministries (ARM), and I regard it as a wonderful privilege to have been allowed to serve in this way. I was permanently dizzy with excitement in my first year, meeting people I had regarded as charismatic superheroes, including Michael Harper, who showed tremendous kindness and welcome to me, particularly in my early and rather naïve days in the job. Of course it was inevitable that I should discover that my superheroes had feet of clay, but this was always more comforting than disturbing, as it spared me the pressure of feeling that I was also obliged to become a superhero! I travelled to most dioceses during my years with ARM and worked closely with many clergy and lay leaders, many of whom were struggling to introduce charismatic life into their parishes, often meeting with strong resistance and anxiety. My experience of charismatic life widened and I learned and experienced much in these years about the powerful effects of intercessory prayer and the reality of spiritual warfare. I also discovered that, in these areas, there was the potential for serious manipulation and a lack of theological integrity. I was editing our house magazine, *Anglicans for Renewal*, and always made sure that each article showed openness and honesty. I also launched *Skepsis*, a theological supplement in which one or two theologians contributed their reflections and research on aspects of charismatic renewal.

At this time, Anglican renewal was becoming increasingly influenced by the Californian preacher and teacher, John Wimber. I was very impressed by his wonderful passion to see charismatic life, especially healing, being expressed in the lives of 'ordinary' people. He took charismatic healing out of the hands of the 'experts' on the stage and placed it where it belonged—in the hands of the people in the pews. For him, a normal Christian life was one in which the power of God could be expressed at any time and in any place, and we should therefore live in expectation of miracles around any corner. This was a very good antidote to the rationalism that still dominated much of the church at that time. Wimber was also very keen on developing the gift of prophecy, and churches up and down the country were growing in expectation that people would hear words from the Lord. A particular expression of this was the use of the 'word of knowledge', in which someone would have an intuitive knowledge about an illness or other condition in another person. Such revelation would provide an openness to healing and information about how to pray for that healing. I am still not convinced, however, that this listening gift is what Paul calls 'a word of knowledge' in 1 Corinthians 12:8; I think it is rather a form of prophetic gifting.

It was inevitable that some parts of the church would mismanage this kind of gifting and there were those who were harmed by very insensitive expressions of charismatic life. Thankfully, Adrian Plass suddenly appeared on the scene with his brilliant *Sacred Diary*, in which the sheer silliness of some charismatic life and practice was exposed. Adrian was writing on behalf of those who had been wounded and manipulated by the wrong use of charismatic experience, and thousands were grateful to him for it.

I think it is probably true that in every Christian tradition there is a kind of 'shadow' side. The spirituality we discover is initially full of light and we feel very positive about it, but then, as we grow to explore it more fully, we can discover aspects of it that are disturbing. This has been true of all the traditions I have explored, and the more deeply I have valued a tradition, the more disturbing and disappointing it is to find its shadows. In the case of the charismatic renewal, which had been for me the source of so much hope and life, it was disappointing to discover that, in some churches and individuals, the way it was used caused more harm than good.

Any of us can have an unhealthy interest in power; charismatic renewal promises impressive spiritual power and therefore carries dangers. In my later years with ARM, I began to grow quite anxious about this interest in power, and kept checking my own spirit to ensure that I wasn't being seduced by it. I was also aware, in an age that wanted increasingly quick-fix solutions, that people could be inclined to confuse the culture of renewal with the real thing. For example, people could come to believe that if you sang the right songs, spoke in a certain way and kept yourself informed with the right books, you would stay renewed. But, of course, at the heart of the matter is our relationship with God the Holy Spirit, who will never be packaged into a particular cultural form. I still thank God for the charismatic renewal, which has done far more good than harm in the church, but I do regret the damage it has done. I recognise that we still need to keep a keen sense of discernment about what is genuinely Spirit-inspired renewal, and what is humanly manufactured.

An important part of our journeying, therefore, is to be prepared to accept the shadow side of the tradition that has come to mean a lot to us. If we have a powerful negative encounter, it is not surprising if that causes us to flee from it; but, if we do this, there is a real risk that we may lose something very precious. Our task is to become truly discerning and to realise that humans can do terrible things even to the most precious treasures. If we have been hurt by a particular tradition, we should ask ourselves whether it was the heart and soul of the tradition that hurt us, or whether it was the way some humans misused it and possibly abused us through it. If it is the latter, we may want to revisit the heart of the spirituality again and see if we can rediscover what we once found of such value in it. Sometimes this part of the journey can only be travelled with a spiritual companion, and healing is needed, but the rewards can be high.

In my travelling of the heart, I see charismatic spirituality as a splashing, sparkling stream—the sort you hear initially from a distance when you are walking through some woodland. The sound gets louder as you approach it, and then you come across a waterfall and watch with fascination the dynamism of the water splashing freely over the rocks and stones until it reaches the bottom. There, some of the water rushes off on its onward journey, while other parts form little pools of still water by the mossy bank. You can kneel down and drink from it, and you can bathe in it and feel its cleansing. All this water has come from the skies in its wild and free way, and is given to sustain us.

John's Gospel contains several pieces of teaching by Jesus about the Holy Spirit, but my favourite is from John 7:37–39:

On the last day of the festival, the great day, while Jesus was standing there, he cried out, 'Let anyone who is thirsty come to me, and let the one who believes in me drink. As the scripture has said, "Out of the believer's heart shall flow rivers of living water."' Now he said this about the Spirit, which believers in him were to receive; for as yet there was no Spirit, because Jesus was not yet glorified.

Many believe that Jesus said these words while the priests were pouring water out around the temple in thanksgiving for God's life-giving blessings. For Jesus, the message was clear: we don't just need physical water to sustain our bodies; we need the water of the Spirit for our souls. Jesus offers to us all the water of the Spirit in the deepest parts of our being. Charismatic renewal is by no means the only way of experiencing this flow of the Spirit, but genuine charismatic life does have the dynamic of water about it. It is full of vitality; it is refreshing and cleansing; it can come as powerful torrents or as still, contemplative pools. Perhaps more than anything else, it can't be organised! In this respect, it is always risky and dangerous—but then, anyone who has chosen to follow Jesus has elected to tread a risky and dangerous road.

Questions for reflection

- What tradition has been your flowing stream? How can you refresh yourself from that river today?
- Has there been an event in your past (like my conference in Nottingham) that held particular significance for you? See if you can go back to it in your mind's eye and recall why it was so important for you. Were the experiences that were significant for you then important for you now? Is there anything you want to recapture?

Jesus, you freely give your Holy Spirit to your people. Lead me to your life-giving streams and teach me to drink deeply of them, so that out of my heart may flow rivers of living water.

Chapter 5

Catholic borderlands

I don't remember when I first became aware of Roman Catholics. I think, for much of my childhood, I made the simple assumption that normal Christians were Anglican. Then I overheard a conversation about a friend of my grandmother who was 'Roman', and this introduced me to the idea that there was another variety of church, different from ours. I noticed that when this Catholic friend of my grandmother was mentioned, voices were lowered as though we were discussing something that wasn't quite seemly in polite company. The feeling I picked up was that this person, though apparently very nice, wasn't properly British. Catholics seemed to belong to another race, and were treated just a bit differently, with a little suspicion. This sentiment appears in an episode of Julian Fellowes' TV series *Downton Abbey*, in which the Earl of Grantham discusses Catholics with the Archbishop of York and declares that he doesn't trust them because there is 'too much of the Johnny Foreigner about them'! This suspicion, which I detected in my parents and has been in the minds of many British people, is, I suppose, another expression of the traditional hostilities that have sadly existed between Protestants and Catholics for many generations.

Then, of course, there were history lessons at school. History was not my favourite subject, thanks largely to the angry and terrifying history teacher at my prep school, but even I, a history dunce, discovered that we as a country 'became Protestant' after the traumas of the Tudor period. I was part of the Church of England, the national church, and others were therefore (so I concluded) somewhat 'lesser' churches and a little less British. This attitude seeped into me without my ever thinking much about it or challenging it. Sadly, I did not have any Roman Catholic friends at that time. At school I had Muslim friends from Pakistan and Confucian friends from Hong Kong, and I enjoyed learning about their cultures and faiths, but Catholics were always a bit of a mystery to me.

In time, of course, I did get to know Roman Catholics; then the door was open through the valued medium of friendship and I quickly shed my old assumptions, but I am left wondering how many Roman Catholics felt this level of suspicion from people like my family members. For many years, Catholics were forbidden to worship in our land, until the Catholic Emancipation Act of 1832. Many Catholics came from Ireland to England and Scotland during the terrible Irish famine of the 1830s and 1840s, so Roman Catholicism started to develop a very strong Irish connection in the minds of the British. With the long history of the British–Irish conflict, and the story of sectarian hatred and violence in Northern Ireland, it is not difficult to see how British people have picked up an instinctive prejudice against Catholics.

When the charismatic movement swept into Britain in the middle of the 20th century, it also influenced the Roman Catholic Church, and this influence was felt right across the world. When I became Chairman of the Kidderminster United Christian Council in the mid-1980s, I discovered a very vibrant group of Catholic charismatics and together we set up some 'Life in the Spirit' seminars that were attended by people from several different denominations. It was undoubtedly the charismatic renewal that broke down any lingering suspicions I had about Catholics and I found a very close kinship with them. In my early days as Director of Anglican Renewal Ministries, I met Charles Whitehead, who has given himself unstintingly to Catholic charismatic renewal over many decades now. He works internationally and his achievements in helping the hierarchy of the Catholic Church to welcome and trust this renewal are extraordinary. The Pope acknowledged his contribution to the church by awarding him a papal knighthood in 2003.[5]

During those years I also met a number of Catholic charismatic priests. One whom I grew to love and respect greatly was Father Ian Petit. He was one of the first of the Catholic clergy in this country to testify to charismatic experience. It was not a comfortable journey for Ian, and I have always thought him one of the most courageous people I have ever met. Opposition to his stand for charismatic renewal was very personal at times and very painful for him.

Sadly, Ian died in 1996, but I was honoured to be invited to participate in his funeral at Ampleforth Abbey on a bright November morning. I travelled up to North Yorkshire with Russ Parker, who had been a friend of Ian for longer than I, and we were invited to robe with a huge company of Catholic priests in the Abbey. We joined them in the funeral procession into the great Chapel and together we remembered our dear, gentle and courageous friend before God. Then we solemnly processed, in clouds of swirling incense lit by autumn sunlight, as the coffin was taken to the silent vault beneath the Chapel and the sounds of the choir singing the *De Profundis* filled the chilly Yorkshire air. Despite the sorrow and solemnity, there was a clear sense of the joyful, flighted Spirit moving among us—the same Spirit who had fired Ian during his life and ministry.

Such friendships as these helped me to see that there is so much more in Roman Catholic spirituality than my hitherto prejudiced views had led me to believe. Yes, there are matters that divide us but thankfully I have learned to live with difference and to form friendships with people who hold different beliefs from mine. Spending time with people whose views differ from ours is an important feature of spiritual journeying. When we have found a spirituality that we love, we can easily settle in its land, keep well clear of the border areas and thereby never encounter anyone who is different. This can create a sense of safety but, for many, such safety can come to feel like imprisonment. I suspect there are quite a number of people whose faith has grown stale and stuffy as a result. They need to find someone from a different part of the country, so to speak, to make friends with them and risk visiting their spiritual landscape, discovering something of their experience of God.

Such encounters carry risk, for sooner or later we will come across a difference of opinion, belief or practice that gives us the uncomfortable awareness that one of us is 'wrong'. In the case of my journeys with my Catholic friends, we have to live with the fact that we hold different beliefs and convictions about key issues such as the nature of the Eucharist. Our personalities will, to some extent, shape how we handle this difference. Having recently been on a training day on the Enneagram,[6] I know I have the kind of personality that is able to hold together difference, but other personality types will find it harder. Nonetheless, the command of Jesus to love one another surely has to mean that, whatever our personality, we are obliged to listen with respect to those whose opinions are not the same as ours.

In my early days as an evangelical Christian, I was given a helpful little book (so I thought) that summarised various sects and heresies, such as Jehovah's Witnesses and Mormons, and it included a final chapter on 'Roman Catholics'. The old Reformation feud between Protestant and Catholic has not completely disappeared in some very conservative Protestant circles, and in my early evangelical days I was happy to go along with the notion that Catholics could not be Christians. How sad it would have been if I had stayed with that view, and kept my distance from Catholics! They have helped me so much on my journey, and perhaps the things that divide us are a kind of pain that keeps us alert and compassionate. To be friends, we have taken a decision not to do battle on the divisive issues. This is not to avoid the responsibility to seek after truth together, but it is to recognise that in God's economy some things will never be entirely clear and there is much that can be achieved for the kingdom by loving one another. In a world that so often descends into bitter tribalism, putting energy into fighting its corner rather than being open to others, Christians have a wonderful opportunity to model a companionship that is about living with difference. As Christian history carries such a shameful story of Catholic–Protestant battles, it is even more imperative that we demonstrate genuine healing and reconciliation.

In my discussions with people about their choice of denomination, I find that doctrine seldom determines which spirituality they choose. Their decision is usually to do with their particular encounters with God and with the people who have influenced them. I wrote to one Roman Catholic friend, Lynda, to ask her about her journey. She wrote about how she had attended both Anglican and Baptist churches, and continued:

A friend invited me to accompany her to Mass in her local RC Church, which I did, one Sunday evening. It has always been rather a mystery what happened to me during that evening, but I had an experience of the closeness of God that was almost tangible. I had experienced this same closeness in a powerful way at the point of my 'conversion' when I was 26, but this was the first time within the context of being in church. I knew nothing about the Catholic Church, the Real Presence, transubstantiation or anything of the tradition of the Church. All I knew was that something different seemed to be there.

I suspect that, for many of us, our choices are determined by experiences such as these. The church where we experience the closeness of God will always be important to us. God has made us all very differently and, because of this, we will each have our own ways of experiencing the closeness of God. For some it will be in charismatic high praise, for others in stillness; for some it will be in freedom from the liturgy, whereas for others it will be in the ritual. And so we could go on.

In the early 19th century, a group of Anglicans in Oxford became anxious about the decline in church attendance, and they felt that one of the reasons for the decline was that the church had effectively become too Protestant. People were not encountering God as they should in their Anglican churches because they lacked aspects of life that could be found in the Catholic and Orthodox churches, and they suffered by being so separated from those historic churches. This group of Anglican leaders started a movement that came to be known as the Oxford Movement (led by John Keble, John Henry Newman and Edward Pusey). It became hugely influential and, before too long, the Church of England broadened its range of worship style and belief—a range that still characterises the Anglican Church today. The Catholic spirituality that became established in the Anglican Church came to be known as 'Anglo-Catholic'.

I learned a little of Anglo-Catholicism through my home church but my experience of this spirituality grew as I offered myself for ordination. It seemed that every person I was required to contact as part of that discernment process was Anglo-Catholic, and, at my selection conference in the old high-ceilinged rooms of the Community of the Holy Name Retreat House in Chester, only two of us were evangelicals; the others were staunchly Anglo-Catholic. I felt such a stranger at that selection conference that I was convinced I would not be selected, so I was astonished when I received the bishop's letter inviting me to train for ordination. I was pleased but anxious. It seemed I would be joining a church where I would always be on the edge, not really part of the family. These Anglo-Catholic associations with the church led me to believe that I was naïve in my theology, inept in my conduct of public worship and not properly Anglican. On the other hand, my evangelical friends led me to believe that Anglo-Catholics were ritualistic in their worship, heretical in their theology and not properly Christian. It was all somewhat confusing! However, I was deeply convinced God was calling me and all I could do was to follow in obedience.

When it came to choosing a theological college, I was encouraged to view St John's College, once based in London but recently moved to brand new premises in Nottingham. I was still at Exeter University when I visited St John's for interview, and I remember that journey vividly. Not long after leaving Exeter, the refreshment car of the train caught fire, and we had to stop at a small station where the offending car was removed and we were allowed a free coffee by way of compensation and reassurance. It was in the early days of the plastic coffee cup with ill-fitting lid. In my attempt to secure the lid to the cup, I managed to collapse the cup completely, and steaming coffee poured over my new suit, purchased specially for the interviews. On the train again, I settled back into the journey, trying to cover my coffee-stained suit with a newspaper. At one point I yawned, presumably in a particularly enthusiastic way because suddenly I found my jaw partially dislocated: I was stuck with my mouth wide open. Eventually I closed it by applying some force to the side of my mouth, but I was not optimistic that my bruised mouth would perform well in an interview situation. Towards the end of the journey, I discovered that I had not kept the vital piece of paper telling me at what station I should alight. Trusting to divine inspiration, I made a guess and guessed wrong, which not only made for a very long walk to the college but also challenged my theology of guidance. The heavy rain that fell on me during the final mile of my journey did have the happy outcome of diluting the strong smell of coffee on my suit, but, even so, I was not in the best of humours when I arrived.

However, I was taken to a lecture by Michael Green, who was then the principal of the college, and, as I sat in the lecture room (initially very conscious of being the only one dressed in a suit and acutely aware of the smell of damp linen and stale coffee), my spirits were soon revived by his presentation. Here was an Anglican priest with the wonderful combination of a brilliant mind and immense enthusiasm for God. While I had enjoyed my theological studies at Exeter, it was a delight to discover at St John's an integrated model of worship, devotion, study and practical application. I had no doubts that this was the college for me. I told one of my interviewers what had happened on my journey, and he said he would offer me a place on the grounds of perseverance alone!

The difficult train journey did, in some respects, feel like the journey on which I was embarking, into Anglican ordained ministry. I felt myself to be something of a passenger, at the mercy of strong influences that I did not understand, which constantly seemed to threaten my progress. In retrospect, though, I think I was in a process of self-discovery, which required regular episodes of disruption to help me assess where I was in that process. It was very clear at that stage of my life that I was not at home in the Church of England, especially the Anglo-Catholic parts of it, but St John's was the place where I discovered that this diverse church was much more homelike for me than I had at first imagined.

I have already mentioned the charismatic and evangelical life of the college, but it was the weekly sessions on spirituality that excited me as much as anything else. Two of our lecturers, Anne Long and David Gillett, were influenced by Anglo-Catholic spirituality and I was enthralled by their lectures on the Desert Fathers and Mothers, medieval saints and mystics, patterns of contemplative prayer and silence, and all manner of things that, in those days, self-respecting evangelicals kept well clear of. Worship became much more important for me during my time at St John's, and I found that the Eucharist became particularly significant. I also loved the late-night Compline service that was run in the candlelit chapel once a week. I found that I hankered after anything that drew me to the holy and the mysterious.

At this time, my father was called in by the Bishop of Oxford to help manage the finances of a rather ailing convent not far from our home in Buckinghamshire. The Mother Superior heard I was an ordinand and invited me to take a private retreat in the convent, so I went along with a mixture of anxiety and curiosity. The convent was a beautiful Victorian building, in its last days of life as a home for its community of ageing nuns. It looked like a set from a Hitchcock film, and I can't deny that I was a little daunted by the long dark corridors, the rattling windows, the silent gliding nuns and the generally austere and damp atmosphere. At the same time, I was rather surprised by the fact that I also loved the place. I loved the sense of prayer, the fragrance of incense that spilled out of the chapel and filled the whole building, and the simplicity of the lives of the sisters who lived there. I only met a few, but those I did meet were full of life and sparkle. I quickly grew to love the great chapel, the sense of holiness in it, the silent meals and the rhythm of the daily offices. Here was a place where I could slow down, find peace and listen to God. I took to going there quite regularly during my two years of training at St John's, during which time it moved to much simpler, economically sensible premises.

This first acquaintance with monastic life meant that I felt quite at home on my ordination retreat at Nashdom Abbey. Those few days in late September were exquisite and I was grateful that it was a genuine retreat, with only a couple of talks and plenty of time for stillness and preparation. Although I was somewhat unnerved by the enormity of what lay before me, I found a strong sense of God's presence in the stillness of this beautiful monastery and the surrounding beech woods, and I heard God's voice speak reassuringly to me about my calling. By the time I walked into Christ Church Cathedral on a sunny and warm morning, I felt a true sense of belonging in the Church of England, and it was my growing acquaintance with Anglo-Catholic spirituality that was largely responsible.

St Andrew's Church, where I served my curacy, was part of the High Wycombe Team Ministry, a relatively new idea in those days. Among other things, this meant that every Monday morning I met with lots of other clergy from the town for a shared Eucharist, a cooked breakfast and a short business meeting. The team quickly made me feel at home. There were only two or three of us who were evangelical; the others were traditional and Anglo-Catholic.

One church in this team was St Mary and St George, and the vicar was Father John Hadley. The word 'Father' caused me some initial anxiety. Only a few days after my ordination, while visiting someone in Wycombe hospital, I was taken aback when one of the cleaners greeted me with 'Good morning, Father'. I naturally assumed she had mistaken me for a Catholic priest, and, until I met John Hadley, I had never heard an Anglican minister being called 'Father'. I was rather against the idea, recalling a staunch evangelical leader who had once pointed out that Jesus had said we should call no one 'father' (Matthew 23:9). I suspected that there was more than one way to interpret that verse, but I still felt somehow uncomfortable with the terminology.

John soon put my mind at rest, however, and it wasn't long before he became a very good friend. When there were parts of Anglo-Catholic life or custom that I did not understand, he would explain them to me and I soon discovered that every part of John's Anglo-Catholic spirituality had been well thought through. He practised no ritual or custom unless he was sure it made sense and had a proper meaning. I was also impressed by his wonderfully compassionate heart. He had a special love for the poor and broken of the world, and in time I came to see that it was perfectly natural for members of his congregation to call him 'Father'. He was young enough to be the son of many of them, but he had a spiritual and pastoral authority that meant people wanted to trust and honour him, and using the term 'Father' was an obvious way of doing this. John was also a passionate supporter of the Campaign for Nuclear Disarmament, and he took me to London on several trips of protest. In those days, Anglo-Catholics were much more engaged in political and social issues than evangelicals, and this again commended the spirituality to me.

I left High Wycombe after Easter 1982. John Hadley invited me to spend my last Holy Week in his parish in Wycombe, and so, for the first time in my life, I immersed myself in the worship and witness of an Anglo-Catholic church. There were services and meetings each night and, as the week went on, the sense of expectation grew. When we came to the Maundy Thursday Communion service, John dressed me up in finery that I never knew existed. I was so wide in my dalmatic (a vestment worn by the deacon at the Eucharist) that I managed to swipe a large vase of flowers over and cause a small flood on the altar steps, much to John's amusement. In the service, we had chanting and foot-washing, liturgy and silence, ritual and incense. After a wonderful Eucharist, someone read Psalm 22 while John gently and carefully stripped the altar of its candles and linen. The sanctuary was emptied of all its glory, until it was left looking cold and vulnerable. We made our way into the Lady Chapel, where the flowers for Easter were being stored, making the place like a lavish garden, dense with the fragrance of lilies. John invited us to imagine that it was the garden of Gethsemane, and there we settled ourselves for the prayer vigil. We stayed in silence until midnight, terribly aware of the story of betrayal and suffering, yet with the flowers reminding us that we were not far from a glorious song of hope.

Never have I been so well prepared in my soul for Good Friday, and, in the three-hour service on that day, I felt that I was journeying as close to my Lord on the *Via Dolorosa* as I had ever done.

On Saturday we came together again at the church, not long before midnight. John had prepared a small brazier by the church porch, around which we gathered. The Paschal candle was lit, and we processed into the church to the accompaniment of Taizé music. There we listened in subdued light to the Old Testament readings of liberation that were preparing us for the glorious news of Easter. Then, at around midnight, John announced the Gloria and, from all over the church, people produced bells, claxons, rattles anything that made a noise. While the organ thundered out in spontaneous musical praise, we all went wild with charismatic abandon, glorifying the God who was risen from the dead. As I write now, 30 years on, I remember the service and that whole Holy Week with a certain wistfulness, as I have never engaged so deeply in the story of the suffering, death and resurrection of the Lord as I did during that week.

What do we need to enable our hearts to open up to a different tradition? The most obvious requirement is a soul friend—someone who knows the territory and can walk with us. For John, Anglo-Catholic spirituality was his home county, and during that week he invited me to explore his home. I was helped greatly by John's respect for me. When we are in an unfamiliar land, we can feel very insecure. We worry about saying or doing the wrong thing. We fear upsetting someone, but, probably more than anything else, we worry that we will end up looking foolish. I wonder how many lands we have failed to explore because we are afraid to look foolish and vulnerable—but in the companionship of a trusted friend, even knocking over a vase of flowers during a piece of finely crafted liturgy doesn't matter. John quickly convinced me that his Anglo-Catholic spirituality was most authentically 'him', but, with his enquiring mind, he also loved to ask about my charismatic and evangelical spirituality. We would often tease each other in the ways that friends who trust and respect each other do. I am so grateful to John for helping me understand his home county. Ever since that friendship, I have felt safer in Anglo-Catholic spirituality, and I have always had friends who are Anglo-Catholic.

While working with Anglican Renewal Ministries, I met Bishop Michael Marshall. He rather reminded me of John Hadley, with his brilliant mind, wonderfully warm and compassionate heart and mischievous sense of humour. Several times I invited him to speak to our national conference and he was greatly loved. Though never a 'card-carrying' charismatic, he was sympathetic and loved the signs of life and the heart for mission that he saw in his charismatic friends. I remember him coming to one conference that was also attended by Bishop Bill Godfrey, another Anglo-Catholic bishop, who at the time was Bishop of Uruguay. Bill presided at an early Eucharist and Michael led the intercessions. It was a beautiful Anglo-Catholic mass that was visited by the

Holy Spirit in a remarkable way: as Michael led the intercessions, we were caught up in such a depth of intercession and song that the prayers went on for half an hour. The liturgy and the gentle leadership of these two bishops took us to the threshold of heaven itself, and there we offered all the pains and hurts of this world that were on our hearts, receiving in return the healing grace of God. People such as John, Michael and Bill have taught me the value of a truly authentic and inspired expression of Anglo-Catholic spirituality to open us up, through the involvement of all the senses in worship, to extraordinary encounters with God.

The word 'authentic' is probably a key for us here. Any spirituality can lose its vitality for a variety of reasons. Its expressions of worship can become hackneyed and stale, and the means of worship can end up as the objects of worship. I have been in fairly lifeless Anglo-Catholic services and I have been in equally lifeless evangelical charismatic services. In this regard, all expressions of worship are vulnerable to the same problem—that of using the forms without giving attention to the real content.

In preparing this chapter, I spoke to a good friend of mine, Trevor Hicks, who has now retired as a priest in the Derby Diocese. For him, the real strength of Anglo-Catholic spirituality is that it is rooted in the corporate rather than the individual. For evangelicals, personal piety has often been seen as a priority, but in the Anglo-Catholic tradition a sense of community is very important. This is expressed in a range of ways, such as the vital importance of gathering together for the Eucharist and saying Morning and Evening Prayer. If it is not possible to meet physically with others, the prayers are still said in the knowledge that thousands of others are saying the same words at the same time. In addition, this fellowship is not just in the present time; there is also a sense of joining in the communion of saints who have gone before us. Trevor Hicks told me, 'I firmly believe that the catholic draws his or her faith from other people, those who have gone before in the great company of saints as well as the present company of saints who make up our congregations.'

This attention to the saints has caused much anxiety among evangelicals but is a source of real inspiration to both Roman and Anglo-Catholics. Of all the saints who are loved, Mary stands out as being the most honoured. Again, evangelicals have grave doubts about such devotion but I have noticed that those who have honoured Mary (and have avoided any sense of idolising her) have found a way to draw a female figure into their spiritual story. Traditional presentations of the Holy Trinity have too often been exclusively male, despite the fact that some references to the Holy Spirit in the Bible are feminine (such as the female dove that descends on Jesus at his baptism in Luke 3:22). But if we go into any Catholic or Anglo-Catholic church, we will soon find a statue of Mary. Stepping past all the controversy for a moment, I can't help feeling that this is the response of the God-created part of our human soul that needs to see the feminine represented somewhere in our worship. We may criticise those whom we deem to be idolising Mary, but perhaps we need to ask the more fundamental question of why they were looking for a feminine object of worship. We, who are made male and female in the image of God, have an instinctive longing to find evidence of the feminine in our Creator. Rather than criticising those who 'worship' Mary, we would do better to look at our understanding of what it means that the God in whose image we are made is both male and female.

One of the rich gifts that Catholic spirituality has traditionally brought to us is an acquaintance with Christian mysticism. At some point on our Christian journey we will probably hear or read about Christians in history whose names have become well known in the area of spiritual life that is broadly called 'mysticism'. Such people are Julian of Norwich, John of the Cross, Teresa of Avila and Meister Eckhart. The language they use is sometimes difficult to understand, and those who write about them can be even harder to fathom. It is clear, though, that some people who have loved and followed God have been drawn into experiences so profound that they are very difficult to write about and explain. The apostle Paul himself seems to have had at least one mystical experience, which he describes in his correspondence with the Corinthian Christians. He uses the third person to describe this experience, but most people reckon he was writing about himself. The experience was so deep and holy that he was reluctant to stake a claim to it publicly. He writes:

I know a person in Christ who fourteen years ago was caught up to the third heaven—whether in the body or out of the body I do not know; God knows. And I know that such a person—whether in the body or out of the body I do not know; God knows— was caught up into Paradise and heard things that are not to be told, that no mortal is permitted to repeat. (2 Corinthians 12:2–4)

Those who have had a Christian mystical experience have often become wonderful guides to fellow Christians travelling through dark and difficult times. It is as if they have seen life in a completely different light, and can therefore find wisdom in some of the most perplexing of life experiences. John of the Cross is a good example of someone who, through personal suffering, experienced a 'dark night of the soul'; yet, rather than dreading or fearing that dark night, he came to befriend it. In his *Ascent of Mount Carmel* he writes:

O guiding night;
O night more lovely than the dawn;
O night that has united
The lover with His beloved,
And changed her into love.[7]

John's experience was that the dark night of the soul led to a completely new discovery of the love of God. He is an inspiration to all those Christian pilgrims who find that their journey takes them into lands shrouded in darkness. Such darkness can be brought about by personal suffering or troubling doubts and lonely experiences of feeling abandoned by God. Christians of every tradition can be subject to these feelings and John is one of the mystics who have provided some footlights for travelling in the dark.

I have found that those with a grounding in Catholic spirituality are often the best tutors for travelling in the dark. The mystics such as John of the Cross own a spirituality that is daringly open to the mysterious. Charismatic spirituality ought to be as open but, in my experience, evangelical charismatics have not been so comfortable with Christian mysticism. The mystics not only give us a deep respect for the extraordinary activity of the Holy Spirit in our lives at any given moment, but they also provide some pathways through the valleys and hard times. They talk about the threefold process of *purgation*, leading to *illumination*, leading to *union*. Purgation is about an experience of suffering in which parts of our lives are purged of impurities, including superficial answers to the problem of suffering. Illumination is the point at which we begin to 'see' in the dark and start to find our way through, often in ways that reason alone would not have given us. Union is the sense of intimacy with God's love, which all humans hanker after. Thus, the 14th-century mystic Julian of Norwich became an extraordinary mentor to a huge number of people who visited her cell during an era of great hardship due to war and plague. Julian received 15 visions that completely transformed her life: she believed that she was entrusted with a powerful message, which was that God's disposition towards all humanity is one of mercy and love—a message that people of her time found hard to grasp in the deepest places of their hearts. It has to be said that human nature has not changed a great deal since her time, as this message is still hard for many Christians to comprehend truly.

I feel I am only on the edge of understanding Christian mysticism, but I notice how many Christians of all traditions are longing to find meaning in the hard times they go through. Trite and slick answers just will not do. Christians can be very taken aback when they have 'apophatic' experiences, in which it is hard to know whether God is present or not, and there are no clear answers. If I am going through a hard time, I find that I am more likely to look to the Catholic and mystical spiritualities for help than the evangelical or charismatic. In my final year working with Anglican Renewal Ministries, I knew something of the journey of the dark night, and it was the mystics who helped to guide me through.[8] I tried to convey something of this message in my talks and writings at that time, but, in the heady days of renewal in the late 1990s, living in the expectation of a great revival, a message about travelling through the dark night wasn't what most people wanted to hear. However, I do see much more openness now, among charismatics, to exploring mystical and Catholic spiritualities, and I believe that in this postmodern and post-Christendom era they have a great deal to say to each other.

I have said that my experience of Catholic spirituality is like being in the borderlands. This is due, of course, to the fact that my home county is evangelical, so I have been instinctively cautious of Catholic spirituality. As I have explained, I grew up believing that Catholic spirituality was essentially unsafe territory. In my journeying, I have had to approach these borderlands and have a closer look. Pilgrim guides such as Ian Petit, Anne Long, John Hadley and Michael Marshall have taken my hand and led me across the borders to explore the regions that have been home for them. There is a sense, therefore, that these are no longer border regions for me, because I can now walk around there without feeling so much like a stranger. In all honesty, there could be parts of the region where I do not feel quite at home. For example, I'm still unsure about such things as the correct ways of genuflecting, how to don certain vestments and how to handle a thurible when censing the altar (to name but a few). Where such things are deemed to be important, my original homeland is quickly revealed. It is as if a foreign accent is detected, and the glances of anxiety or disapproval can make me feel a stranger again. We all need friends across the border to help us understand language and customs that are unfamiliar to us. When God sends us such friends, the borderlands are full of discoveries and, in my experience, great treasures are waiting to be found. The borderland may not be the place where we settle and put down roots, but it may well be somewhere that we frequently want to, and need to, visit for our onward journey with God through life.

Questions for reflection

- What kind of spirituality represents a borderland for you? What has been your personal history with this spirituality: for example, how did you view it as you grew up? What judgments have you made about it in the past? What would help you to explore it further now?
- Who do you know who is at home in this land beyond your borders? Can you spend some time with them so they can tell you about the place that is home for them?

Jesus, you led your disciples into many borderlands of culture and belief. Take my hand today and lead me to the borderland of your choosing. Give me a listening ear and an open heart towards those who dwell in lands different from mine.

Chapter 6

Celtic mountains

When I was offered the post of Team Vicar at St Chad's Church in Kidderminster, I accepted it with great delight but not the slightest thought about the saint to whom the church had been dedicated. I had encountered the name of Chad only once before—at St John's College, where one of the students was a black Zimbabwean called Chad Gandiya. He subsequently became the Bishop of Harare, offering courageous leadership in his homeland which has suffered so much in recent years. This Chad certainly gave me a favourable impression of the name, but until my appointment to St Chad's, Kidderminster, I had not encountered a church dedicated to this saint and had little knowledge about him.

I recall that an elderly woman in the parish had done some research about Chad and, in very neat calligraphy, had written out a summary of his life and achievements, which was displayed in a picture frame that hung near the main entrance of the church. I read the story with only the vaguest interest, because for me, in those days, references to the past were very much beside the point. Life was about engaging in the demands of ministry in the here and now. Too much reference to the 'old days' would only hold up progress, and thus it was that I passed my days in Kidderminster in almost total ignorance of Chad and the vibrant church of which he was such a humble and great leader. Those who come from other traditions of church life might be dismayed at such negligence, but that is simply the way I was at the time. I had heard people referring to 'Celtic Christianity' from time to time, but I considered it rather 'New Agey' and thought that only liberals dabbled in it. It was something that respectable charismatic evangelicals best avoided.

No one was more surprised than I when, only two years after leaving St Chad's, I found myself not only dabbling in Celtic Christianity but becoming an enthusiastic promoter of the thing. I had been working for Anglican Renewal Ministries for a couple of years and was loving the vibrant world of charismatic life. I attended many renewal events in those first couple of years and, in the main, they were inspiring and uplifting. These were the days when renewal in the UK was strongly influenced by John Wimber from California, and, although John took great trouble to understand the British temperament and humour, I found that the cultural expression of much of the renewal I witnessed was North American. Ever since the Azusa Street outpouring, the stream of influence for the culture of renewal has been largely American. While I found myself being immensely grateful to the likes of William Seymour, Graham Pulkingham, John Wimber and others, I hankered after something authentically British. This was because I nurtured an instinct that if we were to re-evangelise these lands, only an expression in the language of British culture would really work. Why should an experience of renewal cause us to move away from our indigenous culture? A British person should not have to become like an American to be spiritually renewed, any more than an American person should become like the British.

Of course, we have seen centuries of colonial styles of cross-cultural mission in which the people who are the objects of the mission have been expected to adopt the styles and culture of the missioners. The proponents of charismatic renewal have had a tendency to follow this custom, such that content and style have become easily confused. My reading of the New Testament has convinced me, however, that when God touches individuals and communities, he does not intend that the people being influenced by this action of the Spirit should become like the messengers of the good news. After all, on the day of Pentecost, many different peoples of different cultures were drawn to the kingdom of God because they heard the disciples speaking in their own languages (Acts 2:11). The disciples were expressing the things of the kingdom of God in the languages of the people, and the Holy Spirit was the inspiration to make this happen. In my thinking, therefore, any activity of the Holy Spirit in renewal and mission should produce this kind of authenticity. If, to become more alive in Christ, I have to adopt ways of speaking and behaving that are not naturally 'me', then something is clearly not right.

So, fairly early on in my time with ARM, I set about searching for a model of renewal and mission that would both fit naturally with British culture and be flexible and sensitive enough to adapt to any culture. As it happened, I did not have to search for very long. The influence I was seeking turned out to be ancient and Irish.

One week in the spring of 1991, my attention was drawn to Celtic Christian spirituality. I had done some work with Ray Simpson, who was then the vicar of an ecumenical parish in Bow-thorpe, near Norwich. Ray had started to share with me his love for Celtic Christianity. At first, I put it down simply to a quirky side to his nature, but in time I came to see that his interest in this spirituality was far from quirky: it was right at the heart of his spiritual life and a powerful influence in the renewal that he was experiencing in the church he led. I therefore asked him to write an article on the subject for *Anglicans For Renewal*, the quarterly magazine that I edited. For some reason, I lost the article when it arrived in the office, and Ray had not kept a copy. This meant that he and I had to work hard to piece together what he had written, and, in the ensuing research work, I found something starting to light up in me.

Around this time, we were invited to run a Day of Renewal in the Durham Diocese and, in preparation for my visit to the diocese, I decided to read a book that David Jenkins, then Bishop of Durham, had just written, called *Free to Believe*. Because David was well known for having radical views, I approached the book with some caution, but in the opening pages my anxieties were pushed to one side as I read about his 'most illustrious predecessor'—St Cuthbert, who is buried in the east end of Durham Cathedral. Just three pages were written about Cuthbert and his beloved island of Lindisfarne, but it was enough to stir me with excitement again. I instinctively knew that I had to visit this island and would find there something significant in my quest for culturally authentic models of renewal and mission.

What was starting to light me up was not so much 'Celtic spirituality' as the stories of the early saints and how they brought the gospel to these islands of Ireland and Great Britain. The likes of Chad were starting to introduce themselves to me in such a way that they were no longer impersonal names attached to churches, but were becoming real people (almost friends) who had inhabited these shores many centuries ago, yet seemed to have lived the kind of authentic, indigenous expression of faith for which I was searching. In my explorations into Catholic spirituality, my guides were contemporary friends that I met in my ordinary walk of life. Here, however, I was finding that my guides were people who had died about 1300 years ago. Of course, friends like Ray Simpson were very important too, but it was the stories of the early saints that really began to inspire me.

I first encountered these stories as I read books by modern authors such as David Adam, who at the time was the Vicar of Lindisfarne. They whetted my appetite for more and pointed me in the direction of an early and great authority on these saints— the Venerable Bede. I excitedly went down to the library in Derby, grabbed his *Ecclesiastical History of the English People* and rushed it back to my study without opening it, only to discover that it was written in Latin! Much to my relief, I quickly discovered that there was an English translation, and then I spent many hours poring over the stories narrated so carefully by Bede. I came across names that were now familiar to me, like Chad and Cuthbert, but I was also introduced to people with nearly unpronounceable names, like Cynigils and Aelfflaed. History had never been my strong subject, but here was a history that felt full of life for me. I found myself meeting men and women who had clearly experienced powerful encounters with God, such that they gave their lives to serve him and to tell others about him.

Aidan particularly impressed me: here was a genuinely humble and lovable man who was at ease with his God, with his own soul and with all kinds of fellow humans. Aidan was Irish and trained in Scotland, but he clearly had a strong call to evangelise the English, and he settled among them and led them to Christ. At first he couldn't speak their language, so the king had to travel with him to act as interpreter (an extraordinary notion in itself). Yet the stories of Aidan give the impression that, right from the start, even when he did not know their language, he was close to the people. He listened to their culture and walked in it. Aidan was just one of many who had come to faith in Ireland during a truly wonderful outpouring of Holy Spirit life in that land and now felt compelled to carry the message of the gospel elsewhere.

As I researched the Celtic saints, other contemporary friends were also discovering life in these stories. By this time, Russ Parker had become a close friend, and it was evident that he too was being inspired by these early saints. Towards the end of this year of fascinating exploration, I was invited to lead a mission to the Anglican chaplaincies of the Côte d'Azur. It did not take me long to accept! I was asked to bring a team, and Russ accompanied me. The team also included John and Jacqui Peet, a couple whom Julia had met during my early months with Anglican Renewal Ministries and who had quickly become good friends. John had taken early retirement from his work in Peugeot and, through an extraordinary and wonderful vision, he had devoted his life to transforming a near-derelict farmhouse and outbuildings into a retreat and renewal centre (now the Redhill Christian Centre, near Stratford-upon-Avon).

Even in November the weather in the Côte d'Azur was warm

and sunny and, on one occasion, we were taken into the foothills of the Alps to a point where we could see Mont Blanc, the highest mountain in the Alps. We stood in silence, mesmerised by the utter beauty of this scene of deep blue, brilliant white and shadows of mauves and greys, delighting in the handiwork of God. It was John who broke the silence. Standing a few feet away from the rest of the group, he stretched out his arm and pointed at the mountain. He then slowly turned in a circle, keeping his arm out in front of him, and as he did so, prayed a Celtic encircling blessing for the lands that lay beneath these great peaks. I had not discussed my interest in Celtic Christian spirituality with John and I had not realised that this spirituality resourced him deeply. I discovered that he had visited Lindisfarne many times, and, as he spoke about the island, I knew I had to visit it with him.

In March 1992, I made my first trip to that holy island. John had hired a holiday cottage there for a week and he kindly invited me to stay with him for a few days. I drove the long journey north on the A1, not really knowing what to expect. A cold wind was blowing and heavy, squally showers slowed the traffic. I wondered what I thought I was doing, spending three days in the cold and rain on a breezy Northumbrian island. However, when I eventually turned off the busy A1 on to the little road that leads to the island, the sun was starting to shine. It was low tide, so the causeway was clear, and as I arrived at the other side of the causeway, there was John standing waiting for me. I stopped the car, he gave me his usual bear hug of a welcome and instinctively we both fell down on to the sand and prayed. By now it had become a beautiful spring evening, so John showed me round parts of the island before darkness fell and we made our way to the Manor Hotel for our dinner.

The next day, the rain returned with some force. I was deter- mined to see the island, so we donned everything we could think of to keep out the wet and strode out, in the gale-force wind, to the island's north-east coast, where the wind and rain were at their most furious. My preferred climate is a Côte d'Azur summer, so I took very little pleasure in these weather conditions, but in those moments of being buffeted by the North Sea storm, I felt an extraordinary sense of contented homecoming. So much of the environment was unfamiliar, yet I felt happy and relaxed because I sensed that I was home.

After some time roaming around the island, we returned to our cottage for a hot bath and a meal, and started to imagine a rule of life that would hold us true to the spirituality that we felt we were encountering in the stories of those like Aidan and Cuthbert who lived and witnessed on this island so many centuries ago. I was the proud possessor of a laptop (a fairly new kind of device in those days), and I recall sitting on the sofa with the heavy machine on my knee, pounding away at the keys as idea after idea came tumbling out of us. In the days to come, we would share our experience with a few others, including Ray Simpson. In many ways this was the early beginning of the Community of Aidan and Hilda. For the next few years I became actively involved in the setting up of the community and still follow its life with great interest.

My way into this tradition therefore began with a particular quest—the search for an authentic model of renewal and mission. In that regard, the momentum for exploring a new tradition was similar to that which led me to charismatic experience. There was a longing within me and an intentional searching. Books and friends played their part once again, and places also became important. The difference was that this time the most significant book was that ancient one written by the Venerable Bede, an eighth-century monk of Jarrow; and, as I have already mentioned, the friends who guided me were not only contemporary ones but also those to whom Bede introduced me, who lived and witnessed in the age just before his.

I have come to believe that we should listen carefully to these questings of our hearts—the longing to find something more, something more authentically me, something with a sense of home about it. My questing into Celtic Christian spirituality gained greater focus when I was granted some study leave at the end of 1993, which gave me the opportunity to do some sustained reading and research and spend more time on the islands of Iona and Lindisfarne. The fruit of this research was my book *Restoring the Woven Cord*, which was published in 1995. It was my second full-length book to be published, and I was far from sure what the Christian readers would make of it. Until that point, there were only a few books on Celtic Christian spirituality on the market, and, as far as I'm aware, none authored by someone from an evangelical background. For many evangelicals and charismatics, Celtic Christianity was still seen as more to do with New Age than orthodox faith and therefore best avoided. For me, as Director of Anglican Renewal Ministries, publishing on this subject represented something of a risk.

I was working at Eastbourne the weekend it was published, and I was asked to go to the BBC studios in Brighton to be interviewed for the Radio 4 *Sunday* programme. I was astonished that the publication of my book should be of such wide interest. There I was, live on national radio, answering questions on Celtic spirituality as if I were an expert on the subject, although it was patently clear that I wasn't. People expected me to have at my fingertips erudite pieces of knowledge such as the dates of Celtic saints, the meanings of particular Celtic patterns and even the fabric of early Celtic coracles. I vowed quickly that I would not become 'Mr Celtic-Expert', as it was very clear that that was not what God had called me to be. Further, with my poor memory, my chance of remembering historical dates and obscure names was remote, so even if I had wanted to sound like an expert, I would have had a hard job convincing people.

As it turned out, those who wanted me to be an expert on all things Celtic were few and far between, but I did discover a huge number of Christians who were delighted to discover a spirituality that they instinctively loved. The book was published again in 2010 by BRF, so I continue to receive correspondence about it, and people often say, after reading this book and other literature on the subject, that their experience is one of homecoming. Celtic Christian spirituality instinctively feels natural for many people. I also received correspondence from people with an extraordinarily wide range of spiritual backgrounds. Among the first to contact me was a group of people from some of the young independent churches. As they read the book, they became excited about the way the gospel first came to these isles, and they were thrilled by the stories of charismatic power that they discovered there. This was a time when postmodernism was shifting a modernist worldview to one side, and many in these young churches were gaining a new respect for the older denominational churches, with their longer histories and a sense of bygone generations.

At the same time, Roman Catholics and Anglo-Catholics were writing to me. I remember meeting one Irish Catholic nun who ran up to me at a meeting and thanked me for the book with tears in her eyes. She had been working in England for most of her life, but, so she said, the book had helped her to own the spirituality that had been in her heart since she was a child. It gave her permission to be herself and helped her 'to come home'. When I wrote the book, I did not have the interest in homecoming spirituality that I have developed since, but I noted how the 'feeling at home' theme was so often part of people's experience, whether it emerged through visiting places like Iona or Lindisfarne, reading a book on the subject, or engaging in Celtic styles of worship.

It soon became clear that this spirituality felt like a homecoming for more than just Irish and British Christians, as people from other countries testified to the powerful draw that it held for them. My first attempt to share my enthusiasm for Celtic spirituality was in the early 1990s, on a visit to Singapore, which had just enjoyed a period of wonderful sustained revival, with the church becoming strongly missional. I thought my listeners would be thrilled to hear about Cuthbert, Brigid, Columba and Aidan, but I was wrong! The blank and puzzled expressions led me to believe that it was best kept in the British Isles and Ireland. However, a year or so later, in South Africa, I met quite a different response, and part of the reason was that there were some strong resonances between

Celtic Christian spirituality and the innate culture and spirituality of many of the indigenous peoples. I was working with Bishop Eric Pike, then Bishop of Port Elizabeth, and he has written very beautifully in my revised version of *Restoring the Woven Cord* about how wonderful it was to discover a Christian spirituality that connected with the local Xhosa culture in which he had grown up. He wrote:

Here was a Christianity that I was experiencing in far-off South Africa, which I have discovered was not new but had deep roots in the Christianity of the Celts between the fourth and ninth centuries. I couldn't read enough and felt that what had been so real for those Celts was what I was living and experiencing among the Xhosa people whom I was now serving. This was a great encouragement to me, as it gave me a sense of belonging and an assurance that I was walking a path which, though it had become overgrown and obscured, was indeed a well-trodden and authentic path.[9]

The response to my book convinced me that one of the gifts of Celtic Christian spirituality is its ability to draw together different spiritualities and traditions. The subtitle of the book is 'Strands of Celtic Christianity for the church today', and, as I often point out in the many talks and seminars that I have delivered on this subject, it is remarkable to look back on the vibrant church that existed in these lands from the fifth century onwards and see a wonderful weaving together of the different strands of catholic, evangelical, liberal and charismatic. Celtic Christianity is not a tradition, like Anglo-Catholicism or evangelicalism, and it would be terrible if it ever became one. Celtic spirituality has the ability to weave together the many different traditions, and in this respect it is a great help to the traveller of the heart, as it can provide a way of exploring new terrains.

I have entitled this chapter 'Celtic mountains' because when I come to think of this spirituality, mountains come to mind—partly because the mountains in the UK are where we can see some of our most ancient rocks. When I lived in Worcestershire, I used to love walking on the Malvern Hills and was always intrigued by the fact that here I was making contact with something very ancient, which gave me a sense of security in a world where so much feels transient. The fact that Celtic Christianity goes back such a long way into our history is comforting in similar ways: it has stood the test of time, it has survived the storms and all the forces that might seek to erode it, and there it still stands.

A mountain can't be domesticated either, and there is a roughness and untamed wildness in Celtic spirituality that I find very appealing. Of course, the height of the mountains is also significant. The first book I read on the subject was David Adam's *The Eye of the Eagle*, in which he wrote that the eagle was one of the Celts' favourite birds because of the way it could rise high above the storms and use its sharp eyesight. The Celts loved to 'see and perceive', to use the words of Isaiah 6:9. Another book that inspired me at that time (and continues to do so) was Noel Dermot O'Donoghue's *The Mountain Behind the Mountain*. The book is a beautiful guide to pilgrims who want to learn to look at creation with the eye of the eagle—to see the movements and messages of the Holy Spirit that lie (not so hidden) in God's good creation.

I resolved never to become a Celtic expert, but I thank God that he led me to discover this particular piece of spiritual landscape. From time to time, I trek back to the mountainsides of this spirituality and meet again those saints of old, learning from the ways they lived and taught and shared their faith, rejoiced in their Saviour and changed a world. I am in no doubt that they will go on inspiring me until my journey's end.

Questions for reflection

- What has been your experience of Celtic Christian spirituality? What appeals to you in it, and what questions do you have about it? If Celtic Christianity is not your 'mountain' terrain, what is?
- Do you sense questions in your heart that might lead you to a deeper search? If you feel called to do more exploration, what do you need to do in practical terms to embark on this journey?

God of the ages, lead me to the rough mountain paths where I can learn new life from ancient stories. Help me to hear my inner questions and questings, and may they lead me to find my true home.

Chapter 7

Liberal marshlands

I know very little about marshlands and yet they hold a fascination for me. This fascination goes back to a book I loved as a child— Paul Gallico's *The Snow Goose*. Published originally as a short story in 1940 in the American *Saturday Evening Post*, it became a prize-winning novel the year after. It is a simple yet beautifully told story of a tender relationship between a disabled artist, Philip Rhayader, who lives in a lighthouse, and a young girl, Fritha, who meets the artist in her attempt to rescue a snow goose that has been injured by gunshot. Together they heal the bird and, once recovered, it has the strength for its long migrations. As the story unfolds, the snow goose returns each year, to the delight of Philip and Fritha. As Fritha grows into a young woman, the love between the couple deepens, yet is always implicit rather than expressed. The story comes to a tragic end when Philip is killed as he uses his boat in the great rescue during the retreat from Dunkirk. I loved the story during my childhood and loved it even more when I saw the 1971 film with Jenny Agutter and Richard Harris. Then, in 1976, an LP was released on which Spike Milligan read the story alongside music specially composed for it by Ed Welch. I can still hear Spike Milligan's rather mournful voice reading the opening words of the book over haunting music:

The great marsh lies on the Essex coast between the village of Chelmbury and the ancient Saxon oyster-fishing hamlet of Wickaeldroth. It is one of the last wild places of England, a low, far-reaching expanse of grass and reeds and half-submerged meadowlands ending in the great saltings and mud flats and tidal pools near the restless sea. Tidal creeks and estuaries and the crooked, meandering arms of many little rivers whose mouths lap at the end of the ocean cut through the sodden land that seems to rise and fall and breathe with the recurrence of the daily tides. It is desolate, utterly lonely, and made lonelier by the calls and cries of the wildfowl that make their homes in the marshland and saltings.[10]

There was little in this description to endear the salty marshlands to me, yet I couldn't deny a strong fascination for this terrain, which was genuinely dangerous and seemed on the surface to have so little to commend it. I did feel that it contained a kind of wild beauty. Indeed, in writing about the bleakness of the place, Gallico adds the telling sentence, 'But sometimes, with sunrise and sunset, sky and land are aflame with red and golden fire.'[11]

Many years later, I discovered another treasure in this wild land of the Essex coast, and that was to do with a Celtic story. In the seventh century, Chad's brother Cedd came to the region, sent by Finan of Lindisfarne to spread the gospel among the 'East Angles'. Today you can visit the ancient church of St Peter-on-the-wall at Bradwell-on-Sea, built on the site of Cedd's Abbey. In the base of the rough altar there are three stones: dolerite, which was brought down from Lindisfarne; gneiss, from the island of Iona; and lias, from Lastingham, the monastery in the north-east that was founded by Cedd. In other words, this apparently inhospitable place has its own beauty and precious wildlife, and has welcomed saints and nurtured the gospel.

I have chosen marshlands as the terrain to represent my experience of liberal spirituality, because for me, at first sight, the terrain appeared desolate and dangerous; yet, with further study and investigation, I discovered that, seen in certain lights, the land is 'aflame with red and golden fire'. When my faith became alive through the Billy Graham meeting and the school Christian

Union, I was soon drawn into evangelical convictions about the inerrancy of scripture and other strongly held convictions that safeguarded my faith. It was a secure world of certainties, in which most things could be settled with a good three-point sermon by a sound preacher. In those days, the great enemy of our faith was not the secular world, with all its temptations of money, sex and drugs, or the challenge of other faiths, or even the great questions such as the problem of pain. The great enemy was liberalism, for it was the 'enemy within'. So-called Christians (as we judged them) were making claims that the Bible was fallible, that miracles were fabrications and exaggerations, and even events such as the virgin birth and the bodily resurrection of Jesus were up for debate. 'Demythologising' was a main weapon of the enemy, as the foundational stories of our faith were callously dismissed as mere myths and fairy tales. For a young Christian like myself, whose faith was very dependent on certainties, questioning and criticism were a serious threat, which had to be challenged.

At school, the main theatre of operations for this challenge was the RE class that I and my evangelical friend, Gerald, attended. This class was taught by the new chaplain who, we discovered to our alarm, appeared to be liberalism incarnate! He was a young priest and, despite being very warm and friendly, by our reckoning he was deeply dangerous and had to be confronted. Thus, in every RE lesson when he dared to challenge a traditional belief, we were ready to confront him, armed with useful books written by well-known evangelical writers. It was during this time that I became aware of two feelings: first, a great sense of unease about Christians fighting each other in this way, and second, resentment at being made to feel unintelligent, out of date and foolish because I held conservative beliefs. It was the latter that kept me battling with the chaplain and all other liberals I encountered, but it was the former that made these contests emotionally draining. Years later, I met the chaplain again. By this time, he had become the vicar of the church attended by my wife's uncle and aunt, and I remember meeting him with a deep sense of shame that I had been so combative in RE lessons. He was typically forgiving and cheerful as I talked with him, and, as we reminisced about the lessons, it became clear that we had both travelled a long way in the journey of our hearts since those sparky encounters.

The next test for me was my university degree in theology. Exeter prided itself on being the most liberal faculty in the country, so I went there with some anxiety. My first essays were a complete disaster and more than once I was accused of mindless fundamentalism. My classmates were a typical mixture. A few of us evangelical Christians did our best to fly the flag, but the rest were either liberal Christians or secular unbelievers who were doing theology for reasons I never quite managed to ascertain. As time went on, some of the evangelicals hit crises of faith, and it was well known in the Christian Union that the 'Theologs' were walking in very dangerous terrain, where, over the years, many had sunk in the swamps of unbelief and lost all trace of their Christian faith. For some reason, though, my faith never felt under threat in those days, and I loved many of the studies, which were spoilt only by the dreaded exams. In time, I developed a certain amount of academic equipment to counter some of the liberal arguments with well thought-through theology of my own, and this felt especially rewarding. I let go of what I felt to be the more peripheral issues, such as literal understandings of the Genesis stories, and it was no problem to me if three people wrote the book of Isaiah rather than one. But certain things were non-negotiable, such as the bodily resurrection of Jesus and the miracles.

Miracles interested me because I was beginning to see evidence of them in my own journey. Not only was I seeing them, but I loved the idea of a world in which miracles happened. A world in which only rational things were possible seemed to lack colour and life. It was far too prosaic, and it was this that offended me most about the liberalism I encountered in my classes at Exeter: the Christianity presented through these lessons appeared dry and lifeless. Of course, it was not the function of the lecturers to commend Christianity: they were sticking to strict academic disciplines. But while I learned to respect these disciplines, I could see a clear problem in divorcing theological study from a living engagement with the God that we were studying. It felt like studying cookery but never eating the meals we prepared. In the case of miracles, therefore, it was easy to argue that a man with leprosy simply could not find a sudden and immediate cure for his illness through one simple word of command. It is, of course, medically and scientifically impossible. The problem was that I was coming across clear evidence that such miracles still happened. I was witnessing lives dramatically changed and healed by the living presence of Christ and I had to conclude that there were powers and influences in this world that defied rational and scientific explanation.

It seemed to me that what was needed was imagination—the willingness to imagine that things could happen in different ways. For me, it wasn't good enough to say, 'Miracles are irrational; therefore they do not happen.' As far as I could see, miracles did happen and continued to happen; therefore we had to reflect theologically on them and work out what they meant. It was difficult in those days, however, to persuade academics to think in such ways. The problem with the scholarship I encountered was that there was very little space for this kind of imagination.

I liked my lecturers and respected their keen commitment to their disciplines, but there were times when I found them very closed. In their grim opposition to anything that smacked of evangelicalism, I sometimes felt that they were as guilty of fundamentalism (albeit of a different kind) as I apparently was. Anyway, despite my evangelicalism, I gained my degree and left Exeter very grateful for the opportunity to study the subject of theology that I had come to love greatly. Generally speaking, for me liberalism was still a boggy and unattractive marshland but it was not nearly as dangerous as I had hitherto been led to believe. I had, in a sense, learned to navigate my way with safety around this terrain, but I had not witnessed much to endear it to me.

It is fair to say that my relationship with the liberal tradition at that time was essentially combative rather than consultative. Once I got to High Wycombe, I started to form friendships with clergy in the team who were of a liberal persuasion, and I was then faced with a dilemma. Here were people I cared for, who appeared to hold radically different views from mine (even about some essential matters of belief) yet were very much alive in their faith. I couldn't caricature them, put them neatly in the 'liberal' box and treat them as the enemy. They became good friends and, once again, it was through the medium of friendship that I was able to explore a spirituality different from my own. For the first time I was forced to respect a tradition that I had hitherto regarded with more than a little negativity. It is particularly difficult to explore a spirituality that you have perceived as one that threatens your own. The risks seem high: are you going to settle for compromise at some stage? Worse still, will you actually give up some of your own cherished beliefs? As some might put it, will you 'go soft'?

I think what happened for me was that I became much more willing to live with mystery. Take, for example, an issue that is a traditional battleground between evangelical and liberal—the virgin birth of Christ. Evangelicals hold dear to the orthodox view that Jesus was miraculously conceived in the womb of Mary without sexual intercourse having taken place. I have never wavered from this view, and much hangs on it for me. Many liberals, however, treat the story more as a parable, with a clear message. To my mind, they hold an unorthodox view and I feel uncomfortable to think of fellow Christians denying a belief that I hold dear. Even writing this now, I feel the beginnings of anxiety. I sense battle lines being drawn, arguments being gathered, scriptures being prepared for the winning of arguments, and prayer meetings being called. For this particular argument, the stakes seem very high: a fundamental Christian truth is being questioned.

The usual course of events, from this point on, is that the argument becomes adversarial and the person with the most convincing argument wins. I don't want to belittle the importance of good, rigorous debate, particularly over such important issues, but the problem with heated arguments is that relationships become damaged by them. Jesus clearly believed that unity was a key priority for the gospel community and he prays for it repeatedly in John 17. We often take this scripture to apply to important 'high-level' issues, like Anglicans and Methodists getting on well together, but I suspect that Jesus had in mind the much more everyday scenario of two Christians who are struggling to agree on fundamentals. He knew full well that the likely outcome when two people disagree on fundamentals is heated debate, high anxiety and the polarisation not only of views but of those who believe in them. In his command for us to love one another, he was guiding the disciple community into a new way of managing conflict—the way of love. The test comes when I have to love someone whose views threaten beliefs that I value deeply. Such a person can feel like the enemy, and, in the world, enemies fight each other, employing whatever means they can to gain victory. However, in the kingdom of God, that is not an option, for we are called to love the enemy (Matthew 5:44).

It seems to me that Jesus expected his disciples to be passionate about discovering truth, and he gave the Holy Spirit to lead us into all truth (John 16:13), but in the community of disciples this questing for truth is not to drive us apart but to draw us into even deeper love for one another. I have discovered the Holy Spirit to be very active in this area. In the case of my friendships with people who hold liberal convictions, little by little I have been healed of my anxieties, so that it no longer feels threatening to listen to liberal views. I have also been healed of past experiences of ridicule and rejection by liberals (just as I hope that the liberals I ridiculed and rejected have also found healing). The Spirit of God has enabled me to enter into deeper friendships with those who are different from me, so I have found a sense of security that has allowed me to listen more deeply. Such listening is a key quality for travellers of the heart. The hardest part of the journey may well be in meeting those whose views are very different from ours, and yet these people may be the ones who can pilot us into new pathways and help us to discover dimensions of God that our native spirituality has failed to do. Travellers of the heart should actually be on the look-out for people who are different, for they are very likely to lead to new discoveries about God.

The friction between evangelical and liberal escalated during the 1970s. In the Church of England, evangelicals were growing in confidence and strength and increasing numbers of those coming forward for ordination were evangelical. Maybe this was why some liberals wanted to become more assertive. In 1977, a book was published with the provocative title *The Myth of God Incarnate*. Various church leaders and theologians contributed to the controversial volume and what many regarded as an extreme form of liberalism was, as a result, being openly promoted in the Church of England. There were robust evangelical counter-attacks, notably a book edited by Michael Green, called *The Truth of God Incarnate*. One of the contributors to *The Myth of God Incarnate* was Maurice Wiles, Regius Professor of Theology in Oxford, who urged Christians to reject an 'interventionist' view of God and strongly denied the possibility of miracles. Michael Green and Maurice Wiles were in Oxford at the same time, and they were also keen cricketers. I played with both of them on a couple of occasions in the Oxford diocesan clergy team. It came as no surprise to me to discover that Maurice Wiles was a tricky spin bowler and Michael Green an aggressive batsman, but I was impressed to see that these two theological opponents clearly respected each other and were often deep in conversation with one another.

All this took place in the final phase of the cultural era that has been called 'modernism', and what concerned me at the time was the development of a liberal spirituality that appeared to be dangerously accommodating to the culture of the age. It was as if some Christians were saying, 'If we insist on believing in such things as miracles, we will just look stupid in this post-Enlightenment, rationalistic modern age. We are losing numbers from our churches and we cannot afford to distance ourselves from the people, so let's recognise that we are no longer primitive believers, that we have "come of age".' It was Dean Inge of St Paul's Cathedral who said, 'Whoever marries the spirit of the age will find himself a widower in the next', and I think those who aligned themselves with the extremes of liberalism ran the risk of becoming alienated in the postmodern age that arrived towards the end of the century.

In the 1980s the warfare continued and came to another head when Dr David Jenkins was appointed as Bishop of Durham in 1984. Many evangelicals were up in arms at this appointment, as he was a man who made no bones about his liberal beliefs. In fact, 'bones' became the operative word when he made his famously provocative remark about the resurrection, in which he referred to a 'conjuring trick with bones'. Although his comments were famously misunderstood, many understood him to be casting doubt on the physical resurrection of Jesus. Not long after his appointment, York Minster was struck by lightning and the roof of the south transept caught fire. Debates then raged, as wildly as the fire, about whether or not this was a sign of divine disapproval at the appointment of such a liberal bishop. The 'official line' was that it was not a sign of judgment. One of the few humorous moments in the whole episode came when one bishop publicly stated that God does not intervene in this way, but added that it was a miracle the fire hadn't spread further. God was allowed to stop the fire but not to start it! For many evangelicals, that comment summed up the view of the leadership of the church—that God was generally kindly and inoffensive and could do things like stopping fires, but he wouldn't dream of doing anything nasty like warning us of the dangers of heresy or even of inflicting signs of judgment on his people.

I was certainly very uneasy at David Jenkins' appointment, but my views changed somewhat when I met him in the early '90s. I have already mentioned how his book *Free to Believe* had unexpectedly touched me, but I was still nervous of meeting him. He kindly agreed to get together with me to discuss the Day of Renewal that ARM was planning in his diocese, so I drove up to Bishop Auckland and arrived at the bishop's official residence, Auckland Castle, described in one article as 'a Gothic country house'. It was both home and office for the Bishop of Durham, and I was ushered into a grand book-lined study with rather ancient-looking leather sofas and armchairs, and tables covered with random piles of files and papers. The bishop breezed in to greet me and asked if I would like some lunch. The self-closing door swung behind him as he left, and some of the papers scattered to the floor in the ensuing draught. He returned a few moments later with a tray of sandwiches and cans of beer and cola. The door was clearly in a mischievous mood, for it swung back on him before he was through, sending the tray of sandwiches and drinks flying across an already chaotic study floor. My first proper acquaintance with the bishop, therefore, came as we scrambled around his study carpet on our knees, collecting the cans of drink that had rolled into all kinds of inaccessible places!

In preparing for the meeting, I had tried to listen to God, and I felt him give me a disturbing idea. In the opening pages of his book, David Jenkins had written of how, before he became a bishop, he was visiting Lindisfarne when he found on the footpath in front of him a playing card lying face down. He wrote of how he knew immediately what the card would be, and he was right. He picked it up and it was the joker. 'My playing card remains a vivid and personal connection with Holy Island for me,' he wrote. 'It is almost as if St Cuthbert dealt me the joker.'[12] Soon afterwards, he was asked to be the Bishop of Durham, and he often referred to himself as the 'joker in the pack'. The story rather moved me and I sensed God saying something about this bishop—that if Cuthbert were to deal him a card now, it would be the ace of hearts, as he was one who was showing the love of Jesus to a wounded world. I was rather taken aback initially at the thought of a 'heretical' bishop being an agent of the love of Christ, but the thought wouldn't leave me. I also had a strong conviction that I should give him an ace of hearts as a gift when we met, and so I set it in a greeting card with the words, 'I believe St Cuthbert would now deal you the ace of hearts as a sign that your love for Jesus will warm the heart of the church.' It sat heavily in my suit pocket as we shared lunch in his study on that day.

I found the conversation remarkable. The bishop was not at all what I expected. Yes, he liked to tease and provoke (especially evangelicals), but his motivation was to encourage people to think. 'I love to ask questions of Jesus,' he said in between bites of a cheese sandwich. 'Evangelicals are very frightened of asking big questions of Jesus, because they are afraid such questions will knock him off his throne. But I know that he is so secure on that throne that nothing I can ask him will disturb him.' As the discussion went on, I realised that my prayerful hunch was right: he had a great love for Jesus and he freely shared it. At the end of our conversation, I rather nervously felt in my pocket for the card, feeling worried that the gift would ruin the warm friendship that had developed in the last couple of hours. I suddenly lost all faith that my hunch about the card had anything to do with God and so, in a rather timid voice, I said, 'Bishop, I am now going to do something which charismatics are inclined to do, and I suspect is anathema to you, and I feel very impertinent offering you this. But I have a card for you which I believe God would want to give you.' To explain the card, I started to mention his story of the joker, and before I could go on he said, 'O Lord, it's not the ace of spades, is it?'

'No, it's the ace of hearts,' I said, and explained why I felt it was an appropriate card for his ministry. 'That's very touching indeed,' he said. 'I shall keep it very carefully.' He placed it on his mantelpiece and brought an end to our discussion with a very warm handshake. As I left the room, noticing a can of Newcastle

Brown resting on some synod papers by the settee, I felt a great affection for this bishop and also felt that he not only tolerated my rather strange gift to him but actually valued it. What became of it, I don't know, but I discovered when I later led the Day of Renewal and met people in his diocese that he was an immensely caring bishop and much loved. I discovered that, during the horrors of the 1980s miners' strike and its aftermath, he was regularly to be found in miners' homes, sipping tea with them and giving them encouragement. He was undoubtedly a messenger of the love of Jesus to people whose lives had become very broken indeed, and although in some ways it offended my evangelical and charismatic sensibilities, I couldn't deny that God was blessing very many lives through his witness. I was having to admit that this liberal marshland had more life and less danger in it than I had supposed.

As the 1990s got underway, the focus of attention in the Church of England was the issue of the ordination of women to the priesthood. A lengthy period of reports, debates and discussions was drawing to an end, and a vote would soon have to be taken. For some evangelicals and Anglo-Catholics, the move to ordain women to the priesthood was a sure sign that liberalism had now got such a hold on the church that it could no longer be viewed as orthodox and they could not possibly stay in it. Many of us welcomed the decision to make women priests, but for others it was a disaster. One such person was Michael Harper, the globally respected leader of the charismatic renewal. I owed much to Michael, not only for his writings, which had so influenced me in my early charismatic days, but also for his kind and wise guidance when I first became Director of ARM. In the early '90s, though, I became aware of a growing burden in his soul about the Anglican Church. He clearly believed the church to be in grave danger. I was often at meetings and events where Michael was speaking, and I found myself growing more and more disturbed by his words. Here was one who had given his life to the renewal of the church, yet he had nothing good to say about it. The church he described bore little resemblance to the church I had also given my life to serving. Where I was full of hope and expectation, he was full of despair and criticism. Michael was very well acquainted with the wider Anglican Church, and certainly the Episcopal Church in the States had espoused a very liberal 'revisionist' agenda, particularly in relation to homosexuality, which was alarming many. Michael developed the conviction that if the Church of England ordained women, it would be such a severance from orthodox faith that he could no longer be part of it. Thus, when the decision was made and some sang in the streets and thanked God that justice had at last been done, Michael packed his bags and moved to the Orthodox Church.

I very much missed Michael's wisdom and passion for renewal and mission, though I didn't miss his depressing view of the church. However, I found that some of the Anglican renewal movements, particularly in the States, became very focused on battling with the liberal agenda. The new leadership of the Episcopal Renewal Ministries in the States (the equivalent to ARM in the UK) became, as it seemed to me, obsessional about this agenda, and thereby dragged the renewal into a particular camp. Friends I knew in ERM left, and I lost touch with the organisation with which I had enjoyed a special friendship. In the USA there have been divisions and breakaway churches, and the battle between conservative and liberal still rages. Of course, we still have much tension in the Church of England as we navigate tricky waters to do with women bishops, and the contentious issue of human sexuality is never far from the surface of church debates.

The moment the subject of homosexuality is raised either at local church level or on the wider debating grounds of synods, you can feel the tension rising and a sense of battle lines being drawn. Values that are important to us are being challenged—by our fellow Christians, no less—and there is a disturbing sense that we could find ourselves pitting brother against brother and mother against daughter (see Mark 13:12; Luke 12:52–53). Liberals will feel that they are championing deeply Christian values of justice, and traditionalists will feel they are championing biblically based Christian orthodoxy.

In seasons of potential conflict like these, we have to choose whether or not to venture into the marshy lands of a particular spirituality that threatens our own. Few of us like conflict, and we prefer to be in a church where we all happily agree on the fundamentals, finding safety in numbers for our opinions. But I have discovered that retreating from those who believe differently from me leaves me not only with a sense of curiosity but also with some anxiety—a kind of awareness of an 'unknown' that I could encounter at any time, which could disturb and threaten me.

Since 2003 I have been the non-stipendiary priest-in-charge of St Paul's, a small parish in Derby. There is a quality about the life of this church that I have grown to admire greatly, and it is something to do with a willingness to respect those who are different from us. Within the church can be found an assortment of spiritualities. Some would regard themselves as evangelical; some wouldn't know what that term meant, as they are either new Christians or well-established Christians who have grown up in a fairly traditional setting and have not seen the need to identify themselves with any particular spirituality. There are some, too, who would feel they come from a more liberal tradition. It is the first time I have been part of a church including such a range of traditions. Because I feel I'm still a bit unfamiliar with liberal spirituality, it is the one that I need to listen to most, so that I can come to a deeper understanding of it.

To this end, I spoke recently to a clergy couple who both regard themselves as liberal. They are good friends; I know they have chosen the liberal tradition with much care, and it has nurtured their faith well over the years. In listening to them, I discovered that at the heart of their spirituality is a longing to discover the love of God, and their tradition has taken them steadily into a deeper awareness and experience of his love. The wife of the couple owns that she does not take literally some of the stories of the Bible (including the virgin birth), assuming that such stories are 'metaphors for the inexpressible'. For me, as I mentioned earlier, the literal meaning of this story is important, but I'm growing to appreciate that the liberal stance, as understood at least by this particular friend, is not a denial of the story and is certainly not meant to ridicule those who do hold to its historicity, but perhaps represents an even deeper respect for it.

My friend writes, 'Prayer takes me to the place where reason, theology and language become irrelevant and I can only surrender to the mystery of God.' This, I think, is where liberal and evangelical could find some common ground. We may spend a couple of hours arguing about the historicity of the virgin birth, and I doubt we would make much progress, or we could spend an hour in devotion and prayer together around the story, letting go of our need to argue the case and becoming open as the Spirit of God leads us into the real truth and message of the story. I appreciate that to write in such a way declares me a liberal in the minds of some, but I am trying to acknowledge the need for those of different traditions to spend time together, not for the sake of putting each other right but for the sake of seeking God together.

For the husband of this couple, the significance and importance of the tradition is not about finding a doctrine that suits him, but about encountering something holy in the church community and its worship and witness. 'I would be very sorry to seem to suggest that all the church needs is a good dose of liberalism,' he said. 'What the church and all its traditions need is a good dose of holiness and love.' He then added that when he witnessed the hostility of some of the evangelical bishops towards more liberal bishops at the Lambeth Conference in 1998, he turned to God and said, 'Dear God, what a load of prats they are!' He said that the divine answer came in a flash: 'Yes, you are probably right; but have you considered what sort of a prat you are yourself?!' It is, I guess, a modern version of Jesus' statement, 'He who is without sin, cast the first stone', but this humorous story reveals a value that lies deep in my friend's heart. Whether we are engaging in these 'battles' or criticising our 'opponents' from a distance, the challenge is to turn the spotlight on to our own hearts and see whether we are responding from holiness or simply 'being a prat', to use his 'theological' language. These liberal friends are intent on developing a holy life that is based on honest exploration and an acceptance of mystery. They can live with unanswered questions and, as far as they are concerned (to use their words), 'liberal spirituality is about putting holiness and love above everything'.

I know full well that an evangelical might read the last couple of paragraphs and have all their suspicions confirmed that liberalism is simply 'woolly'. It sounds too vague, they might claim. Any religion can talk about love and holiness and mystery, so where is Christ and his radical demands of discipleship? I suspect it is true that some liberals have entered territory that is beyond the boundaries of orthodox Christian faith and belief, but I am learning never to make assumptions about someone who comes from a different tradition from mine. As soon as I label someone, I have ceased to have a proper relationship with him or her. When we label someone, we distance ourselves from them, making assumptions about their beliefs and behaviour, based on our own unexamined prejudices.

Nowadays, I find that once I know someone is from a different tradition, I want to spend time with them and listen to them. In the case of my two friends, I know that we will have some dis-agreements about certain articles of faith, but I am in no doubt that I see in their lives an activity of the Holy Spirit and a devotion to Jesus that I find most inspiring. Earlier in my Christian journey, I assumed that the Holy Spirit flowed only down certain authorised channels; I now realise that the Spirit is not to be confined by any channels that we may like to dig for him: he will soon overflow any banks of our design.

In our journeying we are very likely to come across terrain that is our 'marshland'. For me it has been liberal spirituality, but I think that, for some liberals, evangelical or charismatic spirituality will probably be their marshland. Whoever we are, we are likely at some stage of the journey to encounter a spirituality that we instinctively feel to be dangerous, threatening not only what we believe but, to a certain extent, who we are. It is quite understandable that we should want to keep well clear of such dangerous places, but, as I have taken the risk of exploring such terrain, albeit a little gingerly, I have found that the threats are far less than I imagined. Ground that I thought would give way and swamp me may only *appear* dangerous, and may actually turn out to hold my weight quite successfully. The Holy Spirit really is keen to 'lead us into all truth' (John 16:13) and I have sensed his guiding hand showing me the firm paths in this landscape. I also need companions who know these lands, who will neither fear the place I come from nor mock my anxieties about their territory, but will walk with me and tell me why they so love this particular part of the world.

Thus, when I am no longer deafened by my own anxieties or my arguments in favour of my preferred landscape, I can grow to listen to and witness the good of another's terrain and find my way of travelling in it without risk, allowing it to become a resource to me. I can do the equivalent of listening to the cry of the curlew, red shank and wild goose, and marvel at the variety of flora, fauna and other expressions of life in these apparently inhospitable places. And, if I am willing to spend time here, who knows? There may be days when I will see 'with sunrise and sunset, sky and land aflame with red and golden fire'.

Questions for reflection

- What is your 'marshland'—the spirituality or tradition that feels dangerous for you? What has been your main way of learning about this tradition—books, reports, people? In what ways is it a threat to you? What have you found attractive in it?

- Do you know someone from your 'marshland' tradition with whom you could meet? Can you ask them to explain to you why that spirituality has meant so much to them?

Holy God, be my guide and protector in my explorations. May your gracious Holy Spirit lead me into all truth, so that the pathways of my journey may take me to an ever-deepening knowledge of your love.

Chapter 8

Missional coastlands

The spiritualities and traditions that I have explored in the previous chapters have all been defined by the different ways in which Christian people have chosen to express their faith, but another influence—at one level quite separate from the church—has been a very important part of my journey. It is a spirituality formed by our connection with the world in which God has placed us. It is a spirituality shaped by the view from the church porch, out to the vast congregation of people who have no connection with the church and for whom this book is likely to have little meaning.

In the metaphor that I have been using, the land through which I travel is made up of the different terrains of spirituality and tradition. Now I have reached the coast, where the firm securities of church life in its many forms come to a natural frontier. This is not a border between a familiar land and an unknown neighbouring land. It is something substantially different. Here I can step from a secure barnacled rock into the cold water of the ocean, and I come to a mysterious interface. I can turn my back to the sea and look at my familiar homeland, which, regardless of its varied terrain, is generally familiar—but when I look out to sea, everything changes. As I look to the ocean, I see not only a watery world that is quite different from the solid land that has made up my country; if the light is good enough, I might also see a distant land where people speak a different language and come from a different culture altogether. And if I can't see any sign of land, I may simply look at the restless ocean and *imagine* other worlds.

I love the coast but I live in the Midlands, so I have a sense of sorrow that it is always such a long journey to the sea. Perhaps because of this, visits to the coast are that much more special. In recent months, I have walked down a blustery beach in Seaford, in the south of England, and seen the wind ripping off the tips of the breakers and hurling them as spray into a bright sky. I have also boarded an enormous ferry at Fishguard in South Wales and felt the power of a buffeting sea as we ploughed our way through heaving waves to Ireland. I have also stood on a hillside in the Dingle Peninsula in Southern Ireland and watched the evening lights on the calm water of the bay, and felt delight again at the miraculous way in which the sounds of seabirds take flight from the water and travel such distances.

For most of us, the journey to the seaside involves a sense of wonder. For some, the call of the sea is so strong that they, like the great St Brendan, just *have* to set sail upon the ocean, for the land has become like a prison to them. The *Voyage of Brendan* describes the journey of this man who, at the age of 62, felt the call of God to put out to sea with his companions and search the deeps. It was not just the deeps of the sea that he wanted to explore, but the deeps of God, and if you read the *Voyage* you find that it was a part-literal, part-spiritual journey.

Brendan returned transformed and became an evangelist and church planter until he was well into his 90s. For him, there was a strong correspondence between navigating the seas and preaching the gospel. He learned to thrive in the environment of the ocean, and, maybe because of this, he also learned to thrive in the world beyond the church, the world of pagan Ireland. Like so many of the Irish saints, he learned to navigate the spiritual currents of that pagan world, which might have seemed very alien to a well-established Christian but, for him, became familiar and safe terrain. In that world he preached Jesus and planted communities of faith.

It has always been important to me to develop a spirituality that allows a proper engagement with the world into which God has placed me. I see some Christians espouse a language and behaviour that has the effect of drawing them into a Christian ghetto, and I became aware of this in my early days as a believer. If the evangelical world was effectively my spiritual nursery, I developed ways of behaving and speaking that were identifiably evangelical, all of which felt to me, at the time, to be sure signs of growing up spiritually. I would call Christian friends 'brother' and 'sister', would freely use words like 'sin' and 'redemption', and the expression 'Praise the Lord' became like a spiritual burp that erupted at the digestion of every piece of Christian good news (which was plentiful when you lived in a triumphalistic world). When praying out loud in a group, I quickly developed the habit of using those well-worn words 'just' and 'really' and even found myself slipping into the evangelical click—that unsticking of the tongue from the roof of the mouth, usually delivered with a frown, that somehow signals serious intent.

In many ways, there was nothing wrong with this vocabulary and way of speaking but I couldn't help but recognise that it was copied behaviour, which created a sense of belonging in the group. The problem with this, of course, is that such behaviour creates a distance from the people outside the group. I became aware of the fact that I spoke one way when I was in the group, and returned to a different way of talking when I was elsewhere.

I noticed it particularly in my home, which was churchgoing but certainly not used to chatting about God freely at every turn. Religion was best kept as a private matter. If I had come down to breakfast and said, 'Praise the Lord, he gave me a revelation in the night,' my parents would have quickly checked my cupboards for hallucinatory drugs. At the time, I was sorry about the uncomfortable gap that I felt between my Christian world and my family world, but I put it down to the fact that, in my rather naïve estimation, I was spiritually alive and they weren't. I knew the language and they would 'get it' if only they 'saw the light'.

In some ways my new language felt like a liberation. One thing I was very clear about in that world of the 1970s was that I did not want to speak in Elizabethan English, of the sort that I had encountered in church and chapel. I was aware, at this early stage of my Christian life, that it was important to use contemporary language, and I was delighted to come across Bible translations such as the one by J.B. Phillips. My evangelical language was contemporary, and that delighted me, but I failed to see that although it might have been up-to-date English, the way I used it marked it out as the language of a particular culture, which could seem alienating to those who were not part of it. I had assumed that non-Christians would be impressed by my contemporary style. They may have been, but the way I used those supposedly up-to-date words still left me adrift from their culture.

There is a warning here for all who would espouse a particular tradition in the church. Any tradition can become like a club where members adopt certain language and modes of behaviour. The more we mix with people from that club, the less aware we become of how our behaviour and language look to others. All the traditions I have written about in this book are vulnerable to this danger, because it is, to some extent, what humans do when they find a sense of belonging. We are back with the problem of tribalism, where it becomes second nature to adopt the language and customs of the tribe with which we associate. We should therefore have moments when we step back from our preferred tradition and make a serious attempt to take a critical look at how it might appear to the 'outsider'. Surely, the most important thing is not loyalty to our particular tradition but commitment to doing the work of the kingdom of God, that extraordinary kingdom in which all tribes and nations find a place of belonging.

Jesus showed that he had come to preach the good news to the poor, not to reinforce a particular tradition. Where particular traditions threatened to distance people from God, Jesus challenged them. For example, in John 5 we see him challenging the way the sabbath was observed. The spiritual leaders were angry at Jesus' apparent lack of regard for this well-established custom, but Jesus was in no doubt that it served little purpose, except to help the leaders gain power and influence for themselves. Jesus was clear that such behaviour excluded people from the wonderful message of the grace of God. There is, of course, a much longer debate to be had about how we understand the difference between the customs of our particular tradition and core Christian principles, but such discussions should not distract us from regularly questioning our preferred tradition to see if any of its ways are building barriers between the people and their God. Many people leave churches because they become distressed by how far the congregational codes of behaviour distance them from the world in which they live and work and socialise. They also develop an anxiety, even a sense of shame, that their church is so unwelcoming to those who are not familiar with its traditions.

In my early days as a Christian, mission was essentially a very simple notion. Our job was to go out and convert people; once converted, they would delight to come and join our church and behave like us. We held a belief, I think, that anyone whose heart was open to God would recognise religious language and light up. For a time I was encouraged to go up to people and ask them, 'Are you saved?' as a way of beginning a meaningful evangelistic conversation. It won't surprise anyone to learn that I was never given anything other than a blank look in return, or something rather more offensive (which I naturally interpreted as 'persecution'). All the time, though, I felt quite a bit of sympathy for the victims of my predatory approaches. I knew that I would have felt just the same, had I been in their situation. Even at this early stage, I was developing a conviction that people outside the church deserved to be treated with respect and care, and should not be viewed primarily as objects for conversion.

When the 1970s got underway, there was a powerful evangelistic and charismatic movement in the States that came to be known as the Jesus Movement. Thousands of hippies were converting to Christ, and it was fascinating to see that after their conversion they carried on looking very much like hippies, but without the drugs, promiscuity and alcohol. Their conversion did not appear to lead them to adopt evangelical language and customs. A well-known evangelist at the time was Arthur Blessitt, who made a name for himself by carrying his cross around the world and preaching Christ. He had long hair and wore bright shirts, flares and sandals. This was something that upright evangelical Christians in this country did not do! When a good Christian friend of mine grew a beard and wore his hair long, he was roundly chastised for being a 'bad witness'.

Arthur Blessitt was breaking a mould, and I was so impressed by the Jesus Movement that I went to Bromley in Kent to visit a community that was connected with it, called The Children of God. I was keen to see a group of contemporary Christians who were contextualising their faith in their culture. I tentatively knocked on the door and it was opened by a fairly intimidating character who didn't seem thrilled by what he saw—a conventional, clean-shaven, short-haired young man turning up to find out more about the community. However, he invited me in, and several other rather bleary-eyed people of my age joined us. I think most of them had not long been off drugs and the sad effects were still visible. I felt awkward in their company and they seemed mystified by my presence there. The meeting did not last long; then they offered to pray for me, and suddenly I was surrounded by an unnerving mixture of hair and sweat and was terribly disappointed to hear them slip into a way of praying that seemed particularly weird. As it turned out, the Children of God developed into a cult, and even the orthodox believing Christians in the movement never had much impact on society in this country.

I don't think I realised it then, but I realise now that I was genuinely seeking a spirituality that enabled me to live close to

God but also kept me close to the people I wanted to reach. I was reacting against the idea of the church as a ghetto that held a judgmental attitude to everyone outside it and whose only purpose was to drag in new members from a hostile world. Thankfully, at that time I came across the little Christian community in the village of Cuddington that I have mentioned earlier. Their vision was to live incarnationally in their village and to be involved in as much of its life as possible. I therefore found myself shovelling cow muck at the local farm, slicing cheese and ham at the village grocer's shop and joining in Evensong at the ancient church—but at the same time I was part of a very vibrant Christian community.

John and Ros Harding led the community in a way that was refreshingly normal. During this year I saw some amazing conversions, and people were released from alcohol and drug addictions. They celebrated their conversion but still managed to remain wonderfully human. Some of them, from time to time, slid back to their old ways, and we would gather round and try to rebuild them again. I can still vividly remember the warm summer evening when one member of the community returned to the bottle and temporarily disappeared. I went searching for her and tracked her down to a neighbour's garden, where she had slumped among the runner beans. I managed to disentangle her from the beans, netting and bamboo poles and led her home. She was welcomed back in such a loving and unjudgmental way that I remember marvelling at the grace and compassion I witnessed in the community. The prayer meetings (where normal language was employed) were full of human laughter and tears. When non-Christians visited, they were made to feel welcome, not estranged or of less value because they were not signed-up members. I began to see an appealing vision of mission that I could buy into—one that genuinely loved and respected all people, regardless of whether or not they were showing signs of making a commitment to Christ.

By the time I was ordained, therefore, I was fairly sure that my way of missional engagement with the world was to engage as humanly as possible with people, while remaining true to the radical demands of the gospel. From this point of view, becoming a priest was a mixed blessing. On the one hand I delighted in the way my ordination gave me access to people's lives and homes that I had never imagined possible, and it was easy and natural to open up discussions about God with others because that's what they expected clergy to do. Conversely, though, there were times when the dog collar made me feel more distant from people, as they imagined I was much holier than they, or even, in the minds of some, a separate breed of human being.

In my early days of working as a parish priest, I still held the view that 'mission' meant 'evangelism'. When I worked in the Worcester Diocese in the 1980s, there was pressure from some quarters to drop the word 'evangelism' as it was considered to be 'insensitive'. I was told that at one meeting of the Diocesan Synod where this sentiment was strongly expressed, Bishop Philip Goodridge sternly replied, 'But haven't we got a wonderful message to preach? I think we have!' With this episcopal validation, the word 'evangelism' remained in the diocesan vocabulary, but I think I can see why some would have held the opposing view. They observed that parts of the church were focused on evangelising and converting but were not engaging in acts of compassion in their communities or prophetic involvement in society. Back then, social engagement of this sort still tended to be seen by evangelicals and charismatics as rather liberal and not particularly effective, as it supposedly brought no one to Christ. My observation is that this view changed radically during the 1990s, and I believe that what caused this major shift in evangelical charismatic thinking was the so-called 'Toronto Blessing'.

In the mid-1990s, news came through that a Vineyard church situated near the airport in Toronto was experiencing some kind of revival phenomenon. It wasn't long before this renewal arrived in London and thousands of charismatics were influenced by it. As was to be expected, great debates arose over what was authentic and what was not, and the reputation of the movement was hampered somewhat by the fact that those experiencing this renewal often exhibited unusual (if not bizarre) behaviour that some deemed hysterical.

In my view, there were elements of hysteria in some meetings but I was in no doubt that at the heart of the movement was an extraordinary and gracious work of God. One regular 'manifestation' of the Spirit at these meetings was outbursts of laughter, and it was somewhat ironic that the church became seriously concerned by this behaviour. I used to go to meetings of Anglicans and ask, 'Why are you worried about all this laughter? You have been praying for 400 years for the Lord to make his chosen people joyful. Surely you must allow him to answer the prayer at some stage in our history!' But what impressed me more than the laughter and falling over and other curious manifestations was what was going on in the hearts of the people, including my own heart during this time. The church where it all started used as its mission statement the simple words 'Our mission is to walk in the love of God and to give it away', and I have never yet heard a better mission statement for a church. My observation was that the church was receiving an unusual visitation of divine love, and the purpose of this visitation was to put in our hearts such a love for people outside the church that we would give everything we had to care for them.[13]

In evangelical charismatic circles, churches did start to engage in their communities, not in order to convert people but simply because the love of God was driving them to share that love freely with others. Many liberals had been doing this for years, of course, but it is very encouraging to see that in today's vibrant movements for young people, such as Soul Survivor, there is no separation between personal evangelism and engagement in society. Both are expected and they work in harmony.

I could not have been more thrilled to see this happen. I had caught sight of this kind of outworking of charismatic life through Graham Pulkingham and the team from Houston in the early

'70s, and now I was beginning to see it again. A church that greatly inspired me during this time was the Anglican church in Conisborough, then led by Ian Chisholm and whose team included George Fisher and Dave Sherwin. These three found themselves ministering to a community in South Yorkshire that had been devastated by the collapse of the mining industry, working among people who were full of anger and despair. Something happened in that church that no one has ever really been able to explain. There was a most unusual outpouring of the grace and power of God that invaded the heartbroken community.

I was greatly impressed to see that the leaders were completely dedicated to channelling the renewal they were experiencing in the church out into the community. They therefore set up shops and consultancies that helped to restore the town from its state of brokenness. There was plenty of evangelism, not least through Dave's wonderful ministry of going to the pubs and singing all the songs the locals loved (the decent ones!) and then telling them the story of Jesus. The team had such a love for the people that they simply shared each wave of the Spirit of God with the community. It only lasted for a time, as revivals often do, but during those years we were given a vision of how churches can change communities when they engage with them missionally. This church was freely walking in the love of God and delighting to give it away to any who wished to receive it.

Another key influence for me during the 1990s were my visits overseas. I was so grateful for the opportunities to visit churches in other lands where I could witness at first hand how they did their mission. During that time, I visited St Hilda's Church in Singapore, and witnessed the commissioning of a mission team of 40, mostly young people, who were heading off to Sarawak to live with the locals in their long houses (very simple shared homes with no modern amenities) and share the good news. The church in Singapore was sending out about 2500 short-term missionaries to neighbouring countries every year. Their commitment to mission was inspiring.

I also found myself in South Africa, not long after Nelson Mandela had been released from prison, where I met a church that was deeply engaged in the pains and hopes of the nation. I visited Fr Jeremy Sylvester, an Anglican priest who had chosen to live in the little squatter camp of Vlakfontein, where he had been joined by another Jeremy, a retired priest. I still recall Jeremy talking about his mission to heal a people who had been so badly brutalised.

In Kenya I met up with my old friend from college days, Ben Muhalya, who was busy planting churches in the rural villages around Eldama Ravine. In South India I saw what was surely one of the biggest healing events in the world, where over 200,000 people had gathered for a Roman Catholic healing meeting. As we were driven to the centre of the meeting, we saw the lame being pulled along on old pieces of wood, the blind being led, and thousands of God's beloved poor making their way there. We also saw wonderful healings. All these encounters in different parts of the world made a huge impact on me as I witnessed courageous and compassionate mission in some very hurt communities.

Back in the UK, we were becoming increasingly aware that our world was changing fast, with serious implications for the way we engaged in mission. It was Graham Cray who first alerted me to the significance of these cultural changes. In 1995, Graham (then Principal of Ridley Hall, Cambridge) gave a couple of talks that have turned out to be prophetic. He alerted us to the huge cultural gap that was developing between our postmodern world and the church. This rapidly developing culture was becoming less tolerant of a church that appeared dogmatic and controlling. Although the church was making attempts to be 'relevant', these attempts were too often expressed in modernist ways, so the church remained at a distance from postmodern culture. 'We are in an age that is chang-ing drastically,' warned Graham at the conference, 'and in which the old forms of being a charismatic Christian may simply become an ecclesiastical relic. What a fate for charismatic renewal!'[14]

Other voices, such as Lesslie Newbigin, issued similar thoughtful warnings. They found fruition in the *Mission-Shaped Church* report of 2004,[15] which became by far the biggest-selling Church of England report. The group that produced it was chaired by Graham Cray, who by this stage had become the Bishop of Maidstone. The report included stories from across the country of mission initiatives that were taking seriously the changing culture in our nation, and from it came the Fresh Expressions initiative that now includes several denominations.

I have spent some years as the Fresh Expressions Adviser for the Derby Diocese, and, through my contacts in this diocese and through my connections with others working in similar ways elsewhere, I notice that many people are being called into a variety of missional ministries that are very creative and inventive. Some of them are working voluntarily and some are paid. Some are ordained and some are lay. Some are formally recognised as 'pioneer ministers', while others are not, although they clearly have a pioneering spirit.

What I notice about this group of people is that their frame of reference is not the church but those who live and work beyond the church and whose culture would tend to make them feel alienated from the church as it is normally presented. These pioneers are stirred by the question that Bishop Graham Cray has often asked of us: 'Who will fail to hear the call of Christ if we only ever do church in the way that we do it now?' I notice a deep longing in their hearts. They have such deeply missional hearts that if they do too much 'normal' church activity, a pressure builds up inside them that can become intolerable if they are not released for missional engagement with the community they feel called to reach. They are not tied to any particular tradition, and all those I have met are true travellers of the heart: they are willing explorers of different traditions, as long as their work involves missional engagement in some way.

I have also noticed that this has been happening in my own heart, too. Increasingly I find it hard to bear when our church behaves, speaks and expresses its life in a cultural language that alienates those outside. Because of this, my own spirituality is being increasingly formed by mission: I am now more at home in the coastlands and I find I can't keep away from them for long. This, I imagine, is how it was always meant to be. The disciples were in no doubt: they were called by Jesus to make disciples of all nations (Matthew 28:19). They had been trained by him to go out and tell people about the kingdom of God and to demonstrate his wonderful power in this broken world (Luke 10:1–12). After his ascension, he sent the Holy Spirit to them on the dramatic day of Pentecost, and the first thing that came into their Spirit-inspired minds was to get out on the streets and share the good news (Acts 2:1–42). The second immediate consequence of the coming of the Holy Spirit was the forming of a community (Acts 2:43–47). In time, this community came to be known as church, but it was never seen as an end in itself. It was indeed a place of belonging and healing, but it was also vibrant with outgoing life, demonstrating just what the love of God could do among the humans he had created.

The early church was most certainly a missional community, and it was this that inspired the Celtic Christians in the lands that now form the UK and Ireland. The gospel first flourished in such a way in Ireland and then spread to neighbouring countries with amazing confidence and speed. These Christians simply assumed that the faith was for others and that the gospel was profound good news for all people: everyone deserved to hear about Christ. Those who met him and came to life quickly found themselves in a community of disciples and were soon on the road, sharing their faith and building more communities. The early saints did, of course, develop ecclesiology and had their set prayer times and various formalities, but it all seems to have been in the service of others rather than to meet their own needs.

As I write this chapter, I have been sent yet more church attendance statistics that make grim reading for Anglicans. There is no question that we are living in an era of decline in regular church attendance, particularly for people under 40 years of age. There are indeed real points of hope, but we cannot deny that the overall picture is very troubling. Personally I find it much better to own the story of decline than to disguise or disown it. The decline may well be part of a larger work of God that is something to do with the transformation of his church. The American professor of theology Elaine Heath has written, 'The decline is best understood as a corporate dark night of the soul. Because this is a process that the church must go through, it means that the night is initiated by God, and could lead the church to a new and vibrant life.'[16]

Is not the story of death and resurrection at the heart of our faith? I truly believe that the church in the Western world is now in this 'dark night of the soul', and our task is to learn to 'see in the dark', which is what the mystics such as Teresa of Avila and John of the Cross did so brilliantly. Seeing in the dark, which the mystics called 'illumination', is about holding lightly to things of the past that have been precious to us, and having an open heart and mind to the new things that God is doing. It is receiving once again the word first delivered to the exiles going through their own dark night by the waters of Babylon:

Do not remember the former things,
or consider the things of old.
I am about to do a new thing;
now it springs forth, do you not perceive it?
I will make a way in the wilderness
and rivers in the desert. (Isaiah 43:18–19)

This is by no means about abandoning everything old, but it does require a willingness to let go of some of the 'former things' to make space for the new way that God wants to show us. Many of us who work in the institutional church acknowledge that we are working with a 'mixed economy', to use a phrase of Dr Rowan

Williams. The 'new thing' undoubtedly involves God's heart for all people, and the perception of this new thing will have an effect on our own hearts. If we have missional hearts, it will influence the way we view all kinds of church activities.

- It will affect our worship: we will become aware of hymns, songs and styles of worship that alienate others, and so we will look for more inclusive styles of worship, while retaining the sense of awe and mystery that all humans hanker after.
- It will affect our teaching and preaching: we will not be delivering long monologues, because so few people outside the church can cope with this style of education. Our teaching and preaching will be more in the form of dialogue, more graphic, more based on parable and storytelling, and always authentic.
- It will affect our communication: church publicity and other communication will use social networks and other means that are now second nature to many people, especially the under-40s.
- It will affect our fellowship (although even this word is now outdated and 'churchy'). Meetings together may well take place in a pub or other social context, and will include both established Christians and 'seekers'.
- It will affect our nurture of young Christians. Some may not respond to a systematic Christian basics course, but may well prefer something as different as several days of silence in a monastery or convent with a trained spiritual director.
- It will affect our evangelism: while there is no doubt that we have a clear gospel to proclaim, nowadays we have to earn our right to speak, and that usually involves good listening first. There has to be a high degree of authenticity, and we will always need to show that our faith actually works and makes a difference in our lives.

In my experience, all of this is not just missionally more effective but enriches my faith, too. Living missionally brings me into a more dynamic relationship with God and helps me to discern more clearly his heart for this broken world. I therefore have to confess a selfish element: the missional coastland has become a very creative place for me personally. Like Brendan, I watch the shimmering water and listen to the Spirit of God who moves on its face with messages of life and light. I am changed and shaped by those I meet on the seashore and out on the seas, and those I have opportunity to meet from lands beyond this sea. It is a place of spiritual renewal, of life and hope. It is not without its vulnerabilities and insecurities, but it is a place to which many are gathering in our time.

Questions for reflection

- What has been your experience of mission and evangelism in your own journey? Are you happy with the models of mission you have witnessed? Which models impress you?
- What does it mean in practical terms, for you and your spirituality to be shaped by mission? What is exciting about it? What is disturbing?

Lord Jesus, I am your disciple and you call me not only to follow you but to share your good news with others. Give me a listening heart as I meet with those who do not know you, and let me live in such a way that your word of life breaks through in all I do and say.

Chapter 9

Rest and be thankful

In 1803 the poet William Wordsworth embarked on a tour of Scotland with his sister Dorothy and his close friend Samuel Taylor Coleridge. They travelled in a single-horse carriage but took to walking when the roadways became too steep for the horse. In the course of their tour, Coleridge fell ill and had to leave the brother and sister to complete the journey. The two journeyed on the winding road from Loch Long to Loch Awe via Glen Croe. When Dorothy spied a small cottage in the Glen, she wrote in her diary, 'The middle of the vale was a very pleasing object. I said within myself, how quietly might a family live in this pensive solitude, cultivating and loving their own fields.' They climbed up the road that is now the A83, and when they came to the summit they found a seat and a stone with the well-known inscription 'Rest and Be Thankful'. Dorothy wrote, 'The seat is placed so as to command a full view of the valley, and the long, long road, which, with the facts recorded, and the exhortation, makes it an effecting resting place.'[17]

The brother and sister must have sat for some time on this seat overlooking the wild Scottish landscape, for it inspired William to write a sonnet that he called 'Rest and Be Thankful'. It starts by asking who could walk this beautiful road, rest here and not be thankful, and ends with these words:

Nor while the limbs repose,
Will we forget that, as the fowl can keep
Absolute stillness, poised aloft in air,
And fishes front, unmoved, the torrent's sweep,
So may the Soul, through powers that Faith bestows,
Win rest, and ease, and peace, with bliss that Angels share.

In this book I have given a personal account of the different spiritualities and traditions that have been important for me as I have made the journey of life that has been entrusted to me so far. I have imagined these spiritualities as different terrains in the geography of my life. As I stressed earlier in the book, my experience may be very different from others', and by now you may be getting some idea of how your journey looks—what spiritualities you have explored and what the terrains represent for you. You may have thought back to past experiences that made an impression on you. If you are anything like me, when you spend time with some memories and dwell in them for a while, you notice things about them that you didn't see at the time. For example, I found myself surprised that experiences such as the moments of prayer with my old vicar, Stanley Jones, turned out to be so significant. I have also left out many stories that I might have included, and maybe, if I were to start again, I would draw from different memories.

As I recall all these people and events, I feel full of gratitude. Although I thought I was the one seeking new pathways, I find countless signs that the Holy Spirit was beckoning me to those pathways and inviting me into new discoveries. I recognise the importance of adventuring in our spiritual journey, not just settling in one safe place. In this last chapter I want to gather together some principles that I sense are important for enabling a journey through life that not only leads to new discoveries about God but also allows our spirits to grow.

Like Dorothy and William Wordsworth, I pause at my equivalent of the 'Rest and Be Thankful' seat overlooking the landscape. We need such moments of stillness, where we can reflect on the road we have travelled and gain perspective on the terrains that have been part of our lives. As I sit on this bench, I look back at the plains, streams, mountains, marshes and coastlands and find myself reflecting on what gave me the desire, strength and confidence to travel beyond my home county of safety. Such reflection has helped me to identify the following principles, which have been important for me and will probably be important for others, too. In this regard, they offer a simple handbook for travellers of the heart.

Knowing our starting point

It was only as I wrote the chapter on Anglican plains that I began to appreciate fully how deep the Church of England story is embedded in my soul. It seems to me that people may well have mixed feelings about their inherited faith. For some, it has negative connotations. I have met some people from traditions that have been terribly oppressive. Their teachers and pastors of the faith have been at best heavy-handed and at worst abusive. It is not surprising that those who have known such experiences in their childhood want to flee that tradition, as well as the faith it purports to represent. It is very sad that so many in our land won't go near a church because of the way they were treated when they were young. Others, of course, are fortunate to have had a very positive experience, and still others, like myself, have had what could best be described as a mixed experience. Whatever the circumstances, that particular tradition has left its mark on us, and it is helpful to acknowledge this and reflect on its influence on our walk with God and the choices we have made in our journey. As you think about your starting point, you may like to use these reflective questions:

- What do you think has been the effect of your inherited tradition on your life?
- Are you living in reaction to that tradition or in harmony with it?

Letting go

Some of us form close associations with a particular spirituality early in our lives, so that it becomes second nature to us. For example, those brought up on the Book of Common Prayer become so familiar with its beautiful language that the words, rhythms and cadences of the prayers, collects and chants lodge deeply in their hearts, and their identity in God is intimately bound up with those words. For such people, moving into modern forms of worship is painful because it feels as if a very intimate part of their souls is being disregarded. At the same time, using only one traditional form of worship is very isolating for others. Some lovers of traditional worship become quite aggressive defenders of it, and there have been many fights in churches over such matters. But, as we saw in the previous chapter, if we are true travellers of the heart, we have to learn a discipline of holding lightly to our preferred expressions of faith.

To use the Prayer Book as an example, many people have come into new discoveries of God as they have dared to open their hearts and minds to more contemporary language in worship. Similarly, those brought up on contemporary language, with lots of extemporary prayer, have found something liberating and delightful in Celtic liturgies, where real care has been taken in the use of language. The Holy Spirit loves to be dynamically alive in our hearts, and when the styles we have used to express our faith become stale, he loves to come in and disturb us and bring new energy and life. If we fail to do some letting go at these times, we can miss out on so much. It is not about abandoning the old, because we may find ourselves returning to the old from time to time. It is more about openness and willingness to embrace adventure.

Here are a couple of questions that might help you reflect on this principle:

- What are your feelings about the first spirituality that was life-giving for you?
- In what ways, if any, have you moved on from it? How does it feel to look back?

Working with our past

At this resting place, it is appropriate to give thanks for our past, taking the opportunity to look at the road along which we have journeyed. In my case, I have travelled through a number of terrains, all of which have had a clear influence on my walk with God. Sometimes when I look back, particularly to my early days, I feel embarrassed about the way I was and the way I behaved. I read my old journals and feel awkward about some of the language I used, which was far more 'religious' than the language I would use now. Some of my understanding of God looks very naïve and my theology unformed. It's not long before I start to feel a bit ashamed and critical of myself—but I have found it important to stop this process as soon as I spot it happening. There is little point in standing in judgment over our younger selves. Most of us were simply trying to be true to ourselves, follow God and make sense of a confusing world as best we could. As soon as we start judging our younger selves, we start to disintegrate inside.

In the days when I was involved in counselling and inner healing workshops, we put much effort into welcoming parts of ourselves that we had denied or of which we were ashamed. We used cushions to represent those parts of ourselves, and there would often be moving scenes of grown men hugging to themselves the frightened teenager of their youth and giving him comfort. There was no question that the process was very integrating and healing. I have found a similar discipline to be true in our spiritual journey. I have to make friends with that rather strict evangelical young man who was me in my late teens. I have moved on in my journey, but that young man was beloved by God and can therefore be loved by me. I have found that this positive approach to personal history leads to a deeper peace and wholeness than taking an accusing and critical approach. It also makes me far more tolerant of those I meet now who remind me of how I used to be.

Some people, as they think back over their journey, will recall terrains that were distinctly hostile and hurtful for them. For example, some churches in the charismatic tradition have sadly been both controlling and manipulative. Those who have had a traumatic experience will want to avoid that terrain for ever after. Many of us may look back at parts of our journey with regret or pain. In such circumstances, we have to take them to the Lord for his healing touch. I love Psalm 84, the pilgrimage psalm that is about journeying to the temple in Jerusalem. This psalm writer has clearly had bleak times on the journey but has experienced the healing of God, for he writes:

Happy are those whose strength is in you,
in whose heart are the highways to Zion.
As they go through the valley of Baca
they make it a place of springs;
the early rain also covers it with pools. (Psalm 84:5–6)

There is a healing dimension to all pilgrimage, and, in our journey through life, it is comforting to know that God is interested in touching those valleys of Baca (literally 'weeping'), to turn the tears of grief into springs of living water. As you reflect on your past journey, you may like to think about these questions:

- As you look back, are there moments when you feel ashamed of the kind of person you were and the spirituality you espoused? If so, ask God to help you see how much he loved you then, so that you can accept this part of yourself and your story.
- Are there any 'valleys of Baca' in your journey? If so, think about offering them to the Lord for his healing and transformation. How might they become a place of springs for you?

Travelling companions

To explore a new terrain, most of us will need a travelling companion who knows the land and, particularly in the first part of our journey, can act as our guide. I am grateful to God for the companions I have had on my journey. My family took me to an Anglican church where I first became aware of God; a friend invited me to the school Christian Union where my faith came alive; together with another friend I journeyed to a little Pentecostal church and knew that first rush of the Holy Spirit in my life; Anglo-Catholic colleagues and Roman Catholic friends explained the meaning of the sacramental tradition; other friends and colleagues introduced me to Celtic spirituality and introduced me to the 'ancient friends' who first evangelised these isles; more friends and colleagues helped me to understand liberal spirituality, and yet others inspired me with missional vision.

None of my journeying has been alone. Some people will have traversed new terrains through their own explorations, but my impression is that most of us need trusted companions. Of course, we may well be called to be companions to others, to help them navigate a spirituality that is familiar to us but new to them. As you look back on your journey, you may like to consider:

- Who have been your travelling companions? You may like to spend some moments thanking God for them and praying for them. You may even want to write them a letter to thank them.
- Do you know any people who belong to spiritualities different from yours, with whom you could meet and share?

Homecoming

In my book *Dreaming of Home*, I wrote about my conviction that all of us have a kind of homing instinct, a longing to find a place of belonging on this earth, where we can be fully ourselves without fear or shame.[18] Many Christians are restless in a particular spirituality because they don't feel fully at home in it. Such an experience can be particularly disturbing if their church once did feel like home but now feels out of kilter with where they are. People do change and grow and, if the church or spirituality of which they are part is not changing as well, sooner or later there may be a crisis. Although loyalty to a church is commendable, there is no doubt that some people do need to change church and spirituality because they must respond to the call to journey in their heart.

We also have to be aware that, for many of us, no one spirituality will fully feel like home. What's important is to listen to ourselves—listen to what we long for, and listen most closely when we sense a yearning, particularly a 'there must be more than this' feeling. These yearnings and longings can be important motivators for a new time of journeying. We may need to meet with a spiritual accompanier to identify properly what our longing is about and to enable us to explore new directions. While listening to yourself, you may like to consider:

- How much do you feel at home in the particular spirituality with which you currently identify?
- What are you longing for?

Seasons

Some spiritualities may gain particular significance in different seasons of our lives. I have noticed this to be true especially with friends whose natural terrain is charismatic evangelical spirituality. Although there is a very compassionate side to this spirituality and a strong commitment to healing prayer, many have experienced it as lacking if they go through a particularly dark night of the soul, through some kind of grief, a period of depression or serious doubt or a worrying sense of the absence of God. In charismatic evangelical spirituality, much is made of the closeness of God's presence through the Holy Spirit, so a sense of the absence of God can feel doubly disturbing, even shameful.

I have noticed that when charismatics find themselves in a dark night, they often explore Catholic spirituality and can be drawn to convents or monasteries, where they discover healing through a more sacramental tradition. For some, journeying into this new territory provides such comfort and light that they settle there; others return to their more familiar terrain, yet they may try to bring something of their new discoveries with them. These are the people who, as they start to feel stronger, begin to share with their church what God has been doing in their lives through sacramental services (or whatever aspect of other spiritualities they have encountered). The way their church responds will probably determine whether they stick with it or not, but many churches have explored new spiritual territories because they have listened to and respected the journeys that individual members have taken. You might find it helpful to reflect on the following questions:

- How has your spirituality worked for you when you have gone through a hard time?
- What do you need most from a spirituality when you are going through a difficult time?

The problem of tribalism

As we have seen, it is very easy for spiritualities and traditions to become tribal. I have clear memories of anxieties that developed in me at an early age, as I settled into evangelical spirituality. I soon became aware that the evangelicalism I encountered demanded a high degree of loyalty. There were clear perimeters to this spirituality: you were either in the accepted territory or out of it. You strayed out of it when you adopted beliefs that were viewed as unbiblical or unorthodox, or when your behaviour was deemed sinful.

For a short time I quite enjoyed the sense of security that these perimeters offered. Because, in those days, I felt very much in a minority, it felt safe to be in a group of people who believed and behaved in set and ordered ways, so that I knew where I stood. Trusted leaders would come and speak at Christian Union meetings, and we knew they were sound. But my charismatic experience soon pushed me well over the perimeter fencing, and for a short while it felt pretty isolating. Those who had seemed so friendly and welcoming became disapproving and, in one or two cases, hostile. I felt I was being disloyal and betraying a cause. This was a very useful insight into the way any tradition can demand too much loyalty and commitment to the cause.

The same thing happened after I had become charismatic, because I met considerable concern from the charismatic world when I 'dabbled' in Celtic Christianity. In the minds of some, I was becoming liberal and espousing a spirituality that was dangerously new age, thereby corrupting the renewal. I have observed similar dynamics at work nowadays in the Reform and Forward in Faith[19] movements in the Church of England. It is not difficult for such groups to start behaving tribally, so that members find themselves put under great pressure if they disagree or seek to depart from the set ways. I have heard sad stories of people leaving these movements, whose departure has been viewed as betrayal, so that former friends within the movement have become cold.

I have observed all of this not with a view to criticising any particular spirituality or movement, but simply to acknowledge how easy it is for humans, even redeemed humans, to slip into tribal behaviour—and therefore how easily I might fail in the same way. The New Testament makes it clear that the old tribalisms are broken down as Christ builds his kingdom: in this new community 'there is no longer Jew or Greek, there is no longer slave or free, there is no longer male and female; for all of you are one in Christ Jesus' (Galatians 3:28). As soon as we sink into tribalism, we start to dehumanise ourselves, for we have been designed to live as part of a welcoming community.

This is not to say that we welcome a kind of 'anything goes' faith, because clear markers between orthodox and unorthodox faith and behaviour remain important. Throughout the ages, the church has got into trouble by condoning unChristlike behaviour and erroneous beliefs. We need to search our own hearts honestly, exploring our motivations. Where we discern that we are being driven by a need to belong and be in a safe, clearly defined group, we will be drifting away from the vision of the radical gospel community that Jesus initiated.

As you think about the issue of tribalism, you may find these questions helpful:

- As you reflect on your journey, have you been tempted to be tribal in your thinking?
- Where, for you, are the boundaries of orthodoxy? How do you think you can be true to your convictions without behaving tribally?

Those who are different

Our ability to journey to new terrains will depend to some extent upon our feelings about those who dwell in those new terrains.

The difference between the plains and the hills, the dry ground and the marshes, can feel enormous. We may have grown up with lots of prejudices about the marsh-dwellers; we may feel nervous about the hill-people because we have heard they mock those who live in the plains. We may be the children of ancient feuds and warfare, or we may simply feel instinctively anxious in the presence of someone who is different from us. Whatever the causes, it has to be said that Christians have not been brilliant at coping with difference. As I discussed earlier, tribalism may be partly to blame, but if I think of my own journey, it was probably a mixture of factors that made me anxious when I was with those whose spirituality differed from mine.

It was probably during my years with the Acorn Christian Healing Trust that I grew most in this respect. As we developed listening courses, I decided to write one on 'Listening to Difference'. To do this with integrity, I tried as best I could to explore my own soul and discovered that I was fearful of listening to those who were different from me. I was worried that once they knew who I really was, they would in some way diminish me through hostility or mockery. Worse still, they might seriously unsettle me: they might really get me to think! Then I faced the risk that by listening to someone different, I might find myself changing, and that felt disturbing. However, the more confidence I have in Christ to lead and direct me, and in the Holy Spirit to lead me into truth, the more willing I am to engage with those who are different.

This confidence in Jesus is vital if we are to travel to new terrains. When we do, we may well feel challenged in our values, beliefs and customs. For those whose faith is fragile, this may be too risky, and it may be better to wait for faith to grow stronger. But for those whose trust in God is fairly secure, the experience of meeting those who are different can be very rewarding. Of course, we can do this by reading books and articles and watching YouTube, but face-to-face encounters can't really be beaten. Taking an occasional trip to a very different church can be a good idea. Staying after the service and chatting to members of the congregation, discovering what is important to them, can help us to understand what the new terrain is like, and how we might be able to journey in it. After all, Jesus spent time with Pharisees, believers, unbelievers, prostitutes, scribes, tax collectors, priests, Jews and Gentiles. He did not judge people by the labels assigned to them; he had a wonderful ability to look beyond the labelling, to the heart. He surely modelled for us a way of being truly human—a humanity prepared to greet any fellow human, regardless of how similarities or differences. Travellers of the heart need to have this kind of humanity.

Here are a couple of questions to help you think further:

- How do you really feel about people who are different from you?
- What is your greatest fear in encountering difference? Pray about it and ask for God's grace to move beyond it.

Love for others

If you live anywhere in the UK or Ireland and you start on a geographical journey, before long you will reach the coast. In this book I have used the coastlands as the terrain to represent mission, and I think it is true that, as we seek to journey with Jesus, we won't get too far down the road before we reach the subject of mission. At one level Jesus made the faith very simple for us. He gave us just two commands—to love God and to love people (Matthew 22:37–39). His disciples are called to be a community of such radical love that even our enemies are brought into its orbit (Matthew 5:44). At one level, mission is simply the outworking of the commandment to love others: we take the glorious good news of Jesus to anyone who would like to hear about him. If the spirituality we have adopted means that we only ever express our faith in the community of the church, something has gone wrong. God's heart is for his broken world, and we are called to take his compassion, healing and deliverance into this world. I have found that the more I grow aware of this, the more my own spirituality is changed and moulded by this call.

There was a time when I became influenced by a line of charismatic thinking which argued that we can easily be 'infected' by those who are spiritually very different from us. This made me rather cautious when I was with people of different faiths. But it is wonderful to see how the charismatic movement has changed in this regard. Now charismatic Christians are often found in psychic fairs, not waving banners of protest but setting up booths to offer prayer for healing, and chatting freely with the person next door with their collection of crystals.

Particularly sensitive people may be influenced by the spiritual powers that, in my view, are certainly present in these kinds of spiritualities. But I think we are learning that the Holy Spirit is stronger than any other spirit, and love is much more likely to do good to people than fear. As the love of God is poured into our hearts, we will view the person heading into the psychic fair with compassion rather than anxiety or censorship. Perhaps this is happening in all spiritualities as we become aware of God's missional call on us, and so there is really only one question to consider as we think about it:

- With whom does God want you to share his love?

Travelling on

As William Wordsworth sat on the Scottish hillside next to his sister, looking down at the road on which he had travelled and the wide open spaces of the land beyond, he clearly felt a deep sense of peace. He watched the birds in the sky keeping absolute stillness in the midst of the buffeting wind, and he thought of the fish in the streams that he had passed on his journey, which managed to hold still despite the swirling currents. He was no doubt thinking of his normal busy world that might easily push and pull him in all directions, but here at the blessed 'Rest and Be Thankful' place, he could simply ride the winds and the currents and find stillness. What's more, he knew that he was held in this stillness by the power 'that Faith bestows', and that this faith and stillness brought him 'bliss that Angels share'.

Although this book has been about travelling, in the end it is not movement that we seek; it is these moments of stillness—the place of faith to which our journey has been leading. The journey of the heart is a journey towards God: we seek him with our heart, soul and mind. If he is not the goal of our journey, we are very likely to get lost, but if we are seeking him, there is every reason to hope that we will stay on the track that is right for us.

In this book I have hardly mentioned prayer, and yet prayer—that sweet acquaintance with God—is very much at the heart of the matter. Our quest is the deepening of our relationship with God. George Herbert caught this vision of prayer beautifully in his poem:

Prayer is the Church's banquet, angels' age,
  God's breath in man returning to his birth,
  The soul in paraphrase, heart in pilgrimage,
The Christian plummet sounding heaven and earth.[20]

There can be few better descriptions of prayer than his phrase 'heart in pilgrimage'. Travellers of the heart are those who are pilgrims in prayer: although so much of what I have written in this book is about navigating our way through life here on earth, all the time a note is sounding within each one of us, telling us that we travel to an eternal destiny. The peace we know at our resting places is but a foretaste of the eternal peace to come. We have wonderful glimpses of this eternal peace, and every tradition that I have described offers moments when it can lead us into extraordinary revelation, bringing us moments of illumination when the light of heaven shines on our earth.

I shall leave you with a short travelling prayer that you may like to use as you journey on.

May you be led into a voyage of the Spirit
with your heart in pilgrimage.
May you have the courage to explore new lands
and discover their treasures.
May God send you fellow travellers
to guide you to places of welcome.
May you make others comfortable in your land
and, when you visit the windswept coastland,
may God's compassion dwell in you.
And may you rest in Christ
and be thankful.

Notes

1 Eric Pike, *Who Do You Say that I Am?* (Pretext Cape Town, 2011), p. 160.

2 Andrew Jones, *Pilgrimage* (BRF, 2011), p. 198.

3 The Lambeth Quadrilateral comes from the 1888 Lambeth Conference of Anglican Bishops who met in Chicago and wanted to clarify the essentials that bound Anglicans together. These were a) The Holy Scriptures; b) The Apostles' Creed; c) The two Sacraments of Baptism and Eucharist; d) The Historic Episcopate (Bishops).

4 A fuller version of this story can be found in Chapter 1 of Harvey Cox's *Fire from Heaven* (Cassell, 1996).

5 For more information about Roman Catholic charismatic renewal, see http://iccrs.org/ which gives details of the International Catholic Charismatic Renewal Services.

6 The Enneagram is a model of human personality that is principally used as a typology of nine interconnected personality types. It is often used by Christians to help us understand how we behave and how we relate to others.

7 R.H.J. Stewart, *The Mystical Doctrine of John of the Cross* (Sheed and Ward, 1934), p. 2.

8 For more on this story see Michael Mitton, *Wild Beasts and Angels* (DLT, 2000), ch. 4.

9 See Michael Mitton, *Restoring the Woven Cord* (BRF, 2010), p. 188.

10 Paul Gallico, *The Snow Goose* (Hutchinson, 2007), p. 2.

11 Gallico, *Snow Goose*, p. 3.

12 David Jenkins, *Free to Believe* (BBC, 1991), p. 19.

13 For more on this subject, see Michael Mitton, *The Heart of Toronto* (Grove, 1995).

14 *Anglicans For Renewal* Vol. 65 (Summer 1996), p. 7.

15 *Mission-Shaped Church* (Church House Publishing, 2004).

16 Elaine A. Heath, *The Mystic Way of Evangelism* (Baker Academic, 2008), p. 20.

17 Details of this story can be found at www.arrocharheritage.com/HistoryOfRABT.htm.

18 Michael Mitton, *Dreaming of Home* (BRF, 2012), pp. 26ff.

19 Each is a movement within the Church of England that champions a particular understanding of orthodoxy, including, among other things, opposition to the ordination of women to the priesthood. Reform is evangelical and Forward in Faith is Anglo-Catholic.

20 'Prayer' by George Herbert can be found in C.A. Patrides (ed.), *The English Poems of George Herbert* (J.M. Dent, 1974) p. 70.